# THE
# HANDS-OFF
## CEO

# —— THE —— HANDS-OFF CEO ——

**Triple Your Fees** and Profitably Scale
an **Exceptional Consulting Agency**
that Grows Without You

## MANDI ELLEFSON

Unstoppable CEO Press

Hands-Off CEO® and Scale to Freedom® are registered trademarks of Hands-Off CEO, LLC.

Mandi Ellefson
hello@handsoffceo.com
https://handsoffceo.com/

The Hands-Off CEO, Mandi Ellefson —1st ed. ISBN 978-1-955242-58-5

# WHAT EXPERTS ARE SAYING

"What makes this book so different from other business books is the precision-engineered approach to service agencies. It's not the fluff that you see from many out there professing to be business gurus.

Instead, it outlines a process for galvanizing your business one layer at a time so that you have the time and bandwidth to unleash your creativity and expertise. **The result is a business with a strong foundation enabling you to scale, yet still delivers results far beyond any type of productized offering. And delivers results far more consistently than one where the services are reliant on the CEO being involved."**

– Tom Shapiro, Stratabeat, Boston,

Massachusetts

This book is perfect for every agency/consultancy CEO who want to escape the 'hours for dollars' trap and finally have a growing, profitable and purpose-driven firm that smartly removes you from client work and long hours. Mandi's genius solves the three biggest roadblocks every agency owner encounters with a trio elegant solutions that no one else I've ever met has been able to codify or articulate. Her book is enjoyable to read and easy to follow. If you're having trouble profitably scaling your agency, read this book today.

– Timothy Seward * Author of "Ultimate Guide to Amazon Advertising", Founder & CEO, ROI Revolution

"Last year was the highest revenue we've ever made. I am closer now than I have ever been to being a hands-off CEO and sitting in that chairmen seat rather than getting pulled back into trenches. And it's allowing me the opportunity to start to scale up and out of one business and start to leverage that time to get multiple streams of revenue going with other portfolio businesses."

— Wally Waldron, Exitology, Evergreen, Colorado

Working with Mandi has been an essential ingredient for growing myself and my business. Besides the practical input for sales, marketing, developing processes, managing people, growing a company, etc, Mandi has consistently known exactly where and when I needed a (gentle or not) push and/or to give myself permission to be or do what was needed. Her perspicacious leadership is perceptive and always spot-on. The atmosphere of the tribe is the right mix of energy, vulnerability, and always relevant. Without her input, my businesses would not be where they are today and I would not be who I am today.

— Philip Nickerson, P.Eng., Aquatic Production Systems, Nova Scotia, Canada

"Thanks for everything you guys are doing to grow our business. We closed another deal Friday and are **now a little over $44K ahead of all we booked last year (and it's only March)**! Rather than selling one product at a time, our new package enables us to sell a higher level retainer package giving us greater cash flow. Now we're even **selling retainer packages into the six figures.**

*The Hands Off CEO program gives you the tools and systems to make your business more profitable—without you doing all the work."*
– Mark Arnold, On the Mark Strategies, Carrollton, Texas

**"I was working 80-90 hours a week and the work wasn't done.** *I was having to work weekends to catch up. Mandi's approach helped me streamline my operations the rest of the way and actually bring on people to help me with that process. I didn't actually have to do it all by myself.*

**At this point, my business has completely transformed.** *My team has total buy-in. We've gotten to the point where new hires are trained by the other people on my team.* **I didn't actually have to do the training** *and they don't even report to me."*

– Casey von Neumann, serial entrepreneur, Atlanta, Georgia

*"Hands-Off CEO helped me unlock a new level in myself and in my business. They helped us* **increase our rates by 4-5x and have the confidence and commitment to get the right kind of clients and a process to actually deliver solid results** *for them. It has been an awesome growth opportunity of getting rid of that habit of feeling I have to bring in as many clients as possible. And instead just focus on the right ones that are larger, and that are less work. It's been quite transformational."*

– Steven Perchikov, Art of Sales, Miami Beach Florida

*The book gives me direction on what to do because of the examples talk directly to me, it's like this book is written about me! It **gives me confidence and inspiration to want to scale**. As well as ideas and a structure to help solve my pain and problems, it helps me understand this is natural and a common stage in business and I now see there is a pathway through it.*

– Russell Brown, Digital Stream, New Zealand

*"I now have more free time and make **three and a half times more for the work that I'm doing**. And I'm only working with clients who really are the ideal fit for the service I provide."*

– Stuart Trier, Business investor, Kingston, Ontario

*"Working with Mandi not only taught me the difference between working in the business versus on the business, but even more importantly, Mandi taught me to see the world (and thus my business) differently. I've learned just how important mindset truly is when prioritizing long term benefits to the business over short term monetary constraints. **I've learned so much from Mandi and the Scale to Freedom program that I can barely recognize the person and the business I had when I started.**"*

Josh LaMar, Amplinate, Paris, France

*"I was able to cut down my workload, and immediately found 11 more hours per week. Now I have more time to keep growing my*

business and I'm getting my weekends back. The best part is, shortly after starting working with Mandi, I took a long trip away from my business and my team never handled it better."

–Tanya Korpi Macleod, Macleod & Co.

"I was working 60+ hours per week (everyday). Our team was being used in the wrong way and we were burning through good employees. I am now working under 40 hours per week consistently. **I leave my business whenever I want to vacation or to spend time with family, and my team keeps things running without me.**

Having my manager lead this effort gave her confidence and respect for the team so that she could take on more responsibility. I've been able to navigate tricky conversations and empower my team to manage more capacity. This has helped us be more efficient and help the team all move in the same direction. We can now handle more growth without the stress and chaos. It's been invaluable to become more hands-off in preparation for stepping back from my business."

– Michael Marlow, Information Systems of Montana, Helena, Montana

"Working with Mandi helped me get in the right frame of mind to sell my business. It's helped to know the right things I needed in place for my business to be able to run without me so that I could make it more sellable. Mandi helped identify the missing systems and the bad eggs who were causing a lot of headaches in the business, and eating up profits. I learned how to get better work from my employees, and she helped me get the most out of a new operations manager who I promoted.

All this added up to a more hands-off business that could run more without me so that I had time to grow the income from my other business where my real passion is.

Ultimately the work we did together resulted in $10,000 per month of extra profit for my business and a lot less stress for me. The sale of my business is now closing and I am making a lot more from it than I ever thought was possible."

– Randy VanderVeen, Discount Pallets, Grand Rapids, Michigan

"I spent a lot of time growing the business, but I was not sure if the actions I was taking as a CEO were the correct actions to achieve our business goals. It was very stressful. Mandi's Scale to Freedom program gave me absolute clarity on exactly what my role as CEO should be. I was 100% confident that every action that I'm taking will contribute to the company's success. Now we have a very clear program to present to clients, **we've already signed 2 contracts worth $96,000 in the first few months of the program, and I expect our investment will bring us over a million dollars in revenue in the next year."**

– John Moussan, Great White Media, Irvine, California

"**As a service provider you can take steps toward productizing services. But there is a tipping point you can only go so far before you devalue your services.** *Mandi understands the nuance where others like the E-Myth falls short. She has a really good understanding of the next level– a cross between reality and greasing the wheels of operation in a service.*"

– Michael Ziegler, Law Office of Michael A. Ziegler, Palm Harbor, Florida

# Foreword

When I first contacted Mandi, I was working round the clock on what felt like a treadmill that never stopped. There was endless client work. Plus, there was time dedicated to speaking at conferences, writing for industry websites, and even authoring books. On top of all of this, there was the continual need to focus on new sales.

To say I was busy would have been a major understatement.

Our marketing agency was generating strong results for clients. I was extremely happy about that. But the positive impact we were having on our clients' businesses was hiding an underlying problem.

With me so involved in the day-to-day of the agency, we were lacking the systems and processes that would enable us to successfully scale the business.

It's one thing to grow. It's an entirely different thing to scale.

Working with Mandi and her team has been instrumental to both our growth and ability to scale. There are many CEO groups, networks, and masterminds out there. One of the things that makes Mandi's approach so uniquely effective is that she focuses on building an exceptionally strong foundation first. Identifying your most important work. Freeing up your time. Eliminating bottlenecks. Standardizing and streamlining key processes. Implementing more stringent hiring practices. Ensuring that you're strengthening your operations. And empowering your team for success.

Fast forward to today, and we've built a profitable seven–figure business that continues to grow year after year. We're 100% self-funded and have zero debt, with a war chest in the bank.

I no longer need to be so deeply involved in every aspect of the business, as we've built a team of all-stars. For example, we're launching a new business line where although I offer strategic guidance, one of our team members is doing the work and making it happen. And even she has a team assisting her in the effort.

And we've done all of this in a calm, methodical fashion. Everyone eats dinner with their family every day. We don't work weekends. We close the agency between December 24th to the beginning of January every year so that everyone has a real winter break. And everyone on the team enjoys unlimited vacation time. When one employee was faced with fallen trees after a storm, we told her to take the entire week off to deal with it. That's how we roll.

Calm. And focused.

What makes Mandi's book so different from other business books is her precision-engineered approach to service agencies. It's not the fluff that you see from many out there professing to be business gurus.

Instead, it outlines a process for galvanizing your business one layer at a time. From eliminating distractions to making more time for those initiatives that truly move the needle. From removing yourself as CEO from the day-to-day to empowering your employees. From being "busy" to being crazy productive.

The book walks you through a process for standardizing different aspects of your business so that you have the time and bandwidth to unleash your creativity and expertise. The result is a business with a strong foundation enabling you to scale yet still delivers results far beyond any type of productized offering. And delivers results far more consistently than one where the services are reliant on the CEO being involved.

If you're the head of an agency or professional services business and you're finding yourself strapped for time and enveloped in endless day-to-day tasks, this book is for you. Mandi's book is a roadmap for transitioning into a different form of leadership. One in which you refine your focus, build systems, recruit top talent, empower your team, and collectively achieve more.

**Tom Shapiro**
CEO
Stratabeat

# Introduction

## How to Use this Book

There are lots of books on scaling. Some are textbook-like tomes. Others are friendly to small businesses but cover only one individual aspect of scaling. For example, scaling leads, increasing pricing, increasing cash flow and profit, scaling sales, systematizing delivery, creating accountability in the team, etc.

While the focus is good, often, the books are written to be very broad and industry agnostic. Many publishers are looking for mass-appeal books for a larger general readership.

The intention of this book is the opposite. It's narrowly focused on CEOs who have figured out remarkable solutions to painful problems in their industries. They can solve them better than anyone else.

The problem is that it's based upon the knowledge that they've spent acquiring over decades of interdisciplinary training, experience, and testing. It's totally unique to you, so it's very difficult to pass on to someone else.

You have greatness within you that you've had a difficult time scaling with difficult decisions like "Do I take this contract which is going to eat up even more of my time?" Knowing that if you do, it will cut more into your personal life as well.

I wrote this book because this is an overlooked problem that many don't seem to care about.

You're told that if you want to scale, you have to stop working in the business. To most, that means to stop customizing the very solutions that create the impact for your clients that you've built your reputation on. It means stepping back and watching results go from exceptional to just ok.

It often means going down the market and delivering a watered-down version of your services for a client type who just can't appreciate the expertise you're bringing.

In short, to most, sustainably scaling services means becoming mediocre. This book is for those who refuse to accept that as their reality.

You see, I have the same problem in my own business. It means it takes more intentionality upfront to build out the company and mentor my team in such a way as to create sustainability in the company. I am scaling this because the work I am here to bring to the world matters.

Helping the most brilliant service creators in the world scale their ideas and impact the world is my passion. With this book, I hope to help you do the same. It is my sincerest desire that you'll use this book to dramatically increase your fees to overhaul your business into a streamlined profit-producing machine that finally gives you the freedom you deserve!

It is my hope that you'll use what you learn in this book to monetize your brilliance and leverage your past investments to become remarkably wealthy. And that you use your won back time to build up people on your team, to give back to your community, and that you use your growing wealth to bless the lives of others.

In short, this book is my way of scaling my impact by supporting you to change your life and business.

I've spent over a decade testing and proving these frameworks in the book, and I don't dare admit how many years it's taken to finally publish this book. These frameworks won't work for everyone, but they will work for you if you are committed to standing by tangible and valuable results to clients and taking the uncomfortable but effective actions laid out here.

This isn't the easy button. But the rewards are exceptionally rewarding on all fronts for those who choose this path of scaling excellence. The competition is also very sparse because most of your competitors are intellectually lazy. (You know this because you watch them use weak, outdated strategies or take shortcuts that hurt client results.)

How to read this book.

Feel free to skim ahead to get a grasp of the concepts. But this book is meant to be read cover to cover to understand the full big picture. The tactical approach to scaling without looking at how all the factors connect will get you the kinds of breakdowns other experience scaling. They keep growing and dealing with all the old problems without solving them.

If there is just a first name, it's been replaced to preserve their identity. Otherwise, these stories have been shared publicly, and most are on *The Hands-Off CEO Podcast*.

Thank you for coming on this ride. Connect with us on LinkedIn, and don't hesitate to reach out with your comments.

# CONTENTS

# PART 1

## Why Service Businesses Struggle to Scale

# CHAPTER 1

# Overcoming Barriers to Scale

What are you actually building???

You toil away day after day, year after year, giving long hours of your life to your business. But what does your business give back to you?

Maybe a nice income. Flexibility that a job can't give you. But do you actually have the lifestyle you want?

If you're building a custom business services company like a consulting firm or agency, I already know you're working too much. You aren't building wealth as fast as you'd like. Your spouse may be aggravated with you. You miss things with your kids or grandkids. And you've become so consumed with this business that loved ones around you silently (or not so silently) resent *your absence from large parts of their life.*

You keep thinking, "I've just got to get past this next thing... Then it will be better." Then, the busy season ends, and you hire that next person. You get past it, and after the dust settles, it does get a little better.

But then things heat back up again each time a key staffer leaves… Or a client is unhappy… Or you bring on an important account… And you're pulled back in.

Here's how Ryan described what's kept growth stagnant for 3 years in the lower 7 figures:

> *"I started this business as one person with a laptop and cellphone and went out getting clients and making things happen. Eighteen years later, I'm still the hands-on person doing day-to-day chores and calls that aren't really the best use of my time as the CEO. My day gets burned out, and by 4:00 PM, all the things I wanted to get off the list get pushed to tomorrow. My time gets sucked up way too much by tactical tasks instead of strategic tasks."*

The most frustrating part for Ryan was that he could see his company scaling to over $10M if he could just spend more time on growth…

But growth comes at a cost. Milton, who owns a very successful high 7-figure consulting company, continues to experience this cost and put it this way…

> *"I want to be functioning more in the CEO role. But every time we take a little growth step or hire new people, I feel pressure to get more involved to make sure things are happening properly. I'm doing proposals, sales, marketing, financials, and staffing. You know, just about every aspect of it.*
>
> *We got to a point where I was working myself out of that and was able to work on the business— more on strategy and the relationship part of*

*sales. But now that we've grown, I have to be involved in all that again. I am spending chunks of my day on tasks I don't feel comfortable handing off to anybody on my team right now. It was fine when we were smaller, but I'm now pulled back into everything, and I feel like the business is getting a little out of control."*

Milton's story is common. You think more growth will solve the problem, but without the structure (which you'll discover in this book), most entrepreneurs go through a crushing cycle of grow... get sucked back in... question yourself and your ability... grow again... and the cycle just repeats. Most never escape it.

You will be increasingly stuck in your business as it grows or as the market changes. You will need to jump back in to fix things as they break unless you find a better approach to innovate and scale that provides you the freedom you crave and deserve.

Otherwise, you continue paying the very high cost of even more hours of your life and more stress.

You will be pulled into that same cycle, with everyone, including clients, coming at you in every direction, looking to you for answers.

**If you can relate, this book is your wake-up call.**

In this book, I'm going to give you something that no other book about building a consultancy or agency is going to give you. I'm going to show you how to build a *World Class Consulting Agency* that scales– without watering down the innovation and exceptional results that you've built your reputation on.

I'm going to show you how to grow your income, scale your business, and build real wealth.

I am going to show you how to leverage all your previous years of hard work, and how to do it relatively quickly. You'll see how to get free in your business, even if it feels like you're stuck in a business that won't scale.

**If you're happy with the way things are, please put this book down. This isn't for you.**

This book is for you if...

- You're frustrated that you're still working too hard after years of building a team that was supposed to give you more freedom.
- You've experienced the stress of ups and downs in cash flow, and at times even hovered too close to living paycheck to paycheck (and you're afraid to admit it).
- You've at times been forced to rely on the stability of your spouse's employment to fund retirement and cover for the ups and downs in your business.

You've put in your time and worked incredibly hard to get to the success you're at now.

If you're feeling any of those things, you need to know you're not alone, and it's not your fault. My team and I talk with dozens of agency owners just like you every month who started their businesses to chase the dream of wealth and freedom that entrepreneurship promises. Years later, these agency owners find that they're trapped in a prison of their own making.

If you're like most of the owners we talk to, you love what you do and you still believe that it's possible to reach the freedom and wealth you're after, but you might be stuck. I wrote this book as a roadmap to get unstuck. To very quickly get out of jail and build the life you were after when you started.

## Why I'm Qualified to Speak so Boldly

You need to know who you're paying attention to. For the past decade, my firm Hands-Off CEO has supported our clients as they scaled team-led businesses as a vehicle for building real wealth, not just income that comes with the stress of trading your time for money...

But wealth that allows you to truly enjoy the fruits of your labor, have income, make your health a priority, and have time to enjoy it all.

I'm going to show you how to do it through your consulting agency, which is something that most people don't think they can really do. Most people believe that building wealth through a service-based business is virtually impossible because you're trading time for money.

**Yes, you must escape the time-for-money trap, and it is very possible. I know because I had to learn it the hard way more than once.**

My realization that changed everything…

It was a hot Connecticut summer. My family and I had recently moved from Oregon for my husband to attend a medical program. I was nine months pregnant and STILL knee-deep in project work, desperately trying to finish projects before the baby arrived!

Clients had been dragging their feet, not getting me what I needed to complete their projects. My trusted developer dropped off the face of the planet, leaving me with no time to hire someone new and untested. Not to mention, my cash flow was in the toilet because I wasn't taking on new projects with maternity leave looming.

My stress levels were through the roof! We racked up over six figures of student debt, and we were in a new place with no family…completely alone. My husband and I did our best to hold it together, but our relationship was struggling.

The business couldn't run without me, and it most certainly couldn't grow without me.

I am embarrassed to admit that I was trapped to the point where my health had completely eroded– just two weeks from my due date!

I was so stressed that my entire body hurt. My arms were flaring up, and it was all I could do to care for our four-year-old or even do mundane things like driving or using a shopping cart.

I wanted to generate income for my family, but not at this cost. Up to this point, my business was really growing. It had traction, and it was grinding me into the ground.

I'd love to tell you that the story had a happy fairy-tale ending, but that's not what happened.

I made the hard decision to close it down and turn away the new client work that was coming to me. My husband and I decided to make do on less, and I turned my focus to nurturing my new baby and preschooler.

I was frustrated and embarassed. I started the business with the intention of making it able to run without me. Along the way, I built systems so it could grow beyond me. Paradoxically, the last business I managed could run without me for a couple of weeks no problem. I just couldn't translate this to my own company.

**I felt like my business had beaten me.**

Going back to a job was not an option. I had tried the full-time stay-at-home mom thing, and while I loved my daughters, it wasn't a long-term option for me. So I decided to rebuild a business– but better this time.

I began studying others who had the same problems. Before long, common patterns emerged. I was able to help others solve these challenges, and they were happy to pay me for it.

Before I knew it, I'd accidentally started another company, which became Hands-Off CEO. This work quickly became my passion, and I sold my previous company for a pittance to a staff member (who is still happily running it today).

We've since undergone a decade of testing, research, and fine-tuning to uncover the systems and mindsets that build freedom and wealth for service-based business owners.

**What's come out is a proven scaling framework that I needed in my first business, and if you're reading this book, you need it, too.**

We've proven this framework in dozens of consulting agencies. Each time, we scale the agency without commoditizing it, free the owner while building their wealth, and position the firm to attract top clients willing to pay premium fees.

All without the owner working more hours to grow the company.

The Scale to Freedom framework has enabled CEOs to work fewer hours than before (some half as many or less). They've added six figures of profits and created as much as 50% to 100% year-over-year growth as they free themselves to focus on what matters.

The framework gives them relief from a business that would otherwise eat them alive as they grow.

**You need a scaling strategy that drives profitable growth!**

Granular operations systems like *EOS / Traction* are all the rage. These accountability and execution frameworks can transform team output, but without the right scale strategy, your team can become exhausted manually rowing a boat, perhaps in the wrong direction. But an elegant scale strategy built for your model guides a clear direction with the wind in your sails to reach a further destination with less effort. Operating systems are *systems* to execute, not the strategy. No superior execution system will make up for a weak strategy.

Look for a proven scale framework that is battle-tested across many businesses like yours. That can be customized without being cookie-cutter.

*Growing sales and marketing* is not the same as *scaling beyond yourself.*

Scaling growth requires different actions. Advisors without experience in the nuances of scaling service businesses can lead you on an endless treadmill of working harder until you burn out.

## The realities of business wealth building

Those who are the most vocal teachers do not experience true wealth.

We have notable exceptions like Richard Brandson, who owns over 100 thriving hands-off businesses and has immense amounts of time for his personal passions and philanthropic work.

But there's a louder community of voices who preach success at the cost of their personal life. Business growth celebrities tout "turn your 9-to-5 into a 95." Their personal significance is tied up in how "busy" they are, how big their jet is, and how little sleep they need.

**This sick entrepreneurial lifestyle is celebrated like a badge of honor.**

The life of the Hands-Off CEO is doing the internal work to lead an increasingly successful business– without it consuming you. It means finding joy and significance both in the business and outside of your business.

That's key if you want to expand a bigger vision that actually leads to more wealth. The difference is that it comes to fruition through team collaboration. Your productivity and role in the company shift from how much *you can get done personally* to *how much you can get done through others.*

> The Hands-Off CEO movement is about building and mobilizing exceptional leaders who give back with their time, brilliance, and monetary resources to solve the world's biggest challenges.
>
> You become the cause for freedom in your family and your community. You become a force to be reckoned with who

spreads opportunities and abundance with everyone you come into contact with.

In short, I want to give you the power to first transform your own small world, then expand your impact to limitless proportions.

## This is how you build wealth and freedom...

The framework I'm about to teach you is the exact framework I used to become a millionaire in my mid-thirties and continue to use in my business today.

I don't share this to brag, but you need to know who you're getting advice from. You won't see me shooting YouTube videos in rented private jets or rolling up in a Lambo. There's nothing wrong with those things, but for most people, that's not true wealth... that's B.S.

The framework you'll discover in this book will give you wealth, too, but it's about more than just money. Money is actually the easy part. It's about designing the life you truly want to live: living where you want to live, doing the things you want to do, and being surrounded by the most important people in your life– the people and relationships that light you up.

**Here's how I measure wealth:**

**If you stopped working tomorrow, how long could you survive living your desired lifestyle?**

Being able to indefinitely live how you choose and give abundantly aligned with the change you want to see in the world…That's being wealthy!

Ready to start your journey to a business that gives you freedom and wealth? Let's go!

# CHAPTER 2

# I'm Too Busy Working in My Business

*"I successfully sold past businesses, but I worked 60-plus hours a week to get there. Hands-off growth requires a real paradigm shift for me."*

– Serial entrepreneur

As entrepreneurs, we all have a deep desire to win.

We get caught in limbo between growing the business and having the lifestyle that we want.

It can stop us from allowing ourselves to go after all the opportunity that's there because the cost of our current approach to growth is so high.

Maybe the business can run without you for a week or two, but the business can't grow without you. This can feel at times like you're having to constantly feed the alligator so it doesn't come and eat you.

You don't really want a business like this, and neither will an investor if you ever hope to sell. The same things that make your company attractive to an investor will turn your business into a lucrative cash cow that you may never want to sell because owning it is so rewarding.

Many service entrepreneurs think that unless you're in the business hands-on, driving things forward, nothing moves.

My Dad was living that reality.

He co-founded a very successful company that quickly became the second largest in their specialty niche in Canada. However, the company was dependent on him, and the overwork and stress made It unsustainable to keep up. My dad decided to sell his ownership in the business and enter early retirement.

He retired wealthy, but it was at the cost of his health and well-being. It may have even contributed to a mild heart attack in his fifties. He couldn't find the balance and was compelled to choose retirement because of the stress.

He was either on or off. And being *on* was no longer worth it.

You don't have to sacrifice your health to turn your business into a lucrative asset and fund an abundant retirement. You don't have to diminish your vision because you're afraid of what it will take to achieve it. And you don't have to sacrifice your lifestyle and your family to scale a thriving business.

CEOs get trapped in the energy-draining cycle of being overworked and stressed out. They believe the LIE that you have to work harder to make more money. Actually, the reverse is true.

## What if the stress of working so hard is actually slowing down growth?

What if working less actually allows you to not only have more freedom, but to make more money and build more wealth, too?

The sad reality is that most consulting agencies and service-based business owners are trapped by their own success. They spend so much of their time working in their business and have no time to work on their business.

They really enjoy the work they do in the business, but it isn't sustainable.

One consulting company founder described the early multi-million dollar stage as the most stressful because all the biggest problems escalated to him to solve– and it only got worse as the business grew.

He loved his business but hated what his day-to-day looked like. All the fun and energizing activities had been replaced by fighting endless fires. The only way to get to the fun stuff was to work even more hours, which he was just no longer willing to do.

So he decided to quit those parts of the business and retire from doing BS work that wasn't for him.

At a certain point, we need to untrap ourselves from the pressure that lands squarely on our shoulders as the CEO.

## Have you ever had to push-start a car?

When I was in college, my fiancé (now husband) and I drove to Las Vegas so I could meet his parents for the first time. We drove his beat-up white two-door Nissan Sentra with a broken starter, so we had to push start his car all the way from Idaho to Nevada. It was a ridiculous but fun memory.

The 'Entrapment Cycle' is very much like push-starting a car. It's like running back and forth between pushing the car and jumping in to pop the clutch.

It's an exhausting process to keep the car going. But to fix the problem, you have to actually stop the car to replace the starter. The problem is that even if you know how to fix the problem in your business, it's hard to fix because it is constantly in motion.

This is a common pattern that we observe in service businesses stuck in the *Entrapment Growth Model™*.

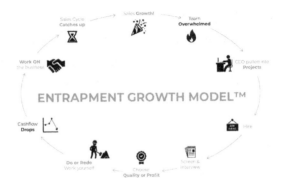

- Sales growth happens.
- The team gets overwhelmed.
- The CEO is pulled into the new projects you just sold.
- You hire to create capacity.
- You endure the long process of screening and interviewing for the new positions.
- You hope you have the right fit, but you're faced with a dilemma: do you work within your budget or pay more and cut into profit? You have to pay yourself and meet payroll.
- So you fill in the gaps by doing or redoing work yourself.
- Growth stagnates, and cash flow drops.
- You go back to working on the business.
- Referrals bring in more work, and the sales cycle catches up, but it's not exactly the best kind of work. Then the cycle starts all over again.

There's this dynamic where you need to hire more experts to help you deliver the growth, but you need more cash flow to be able to hire them. You need more sales to generate more cash, but you need more capacity to make sales without fear of quality slipping.

You're stuck in a Catch-22.

You know there's a ton of opportunity, but you don't have the time to go after the kind of business that's the most profitable and sustainable to deliver.

So you settle for the work that comes in the door from referrals or luck. It brings in cash, and it keeps the team busy, but you're not really getting anywhere. Because you're not attracting the right kind of high-profit clients you need (and just taking what shows up), revenues and profits stagnate, or worse, backslide, as you are pulled into an overload of custom work that you can't fully delegate.

## The cycle traps you in a time-for-money business model

You have the obligations of managing a team, leading a team, meeting payroll, and all the rest... AND you're stuck in this time-for-money model where the only way that you can make more money is to *personally work more hours*.

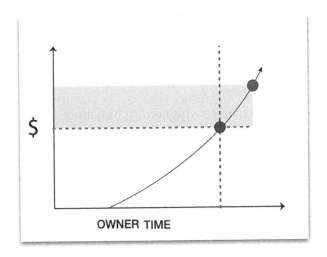

Notice in the '*Entrapment Cycle*™' how income growth stalls as a result of growth being tied to the owner's time.

It's a dead end that doesn't scale, and worse, it grinds you down over time.

## This isn't just about growth for growth's sake.

This is about building a business that can sustain your lifestyle for the long term. If you're anything like the overwhelming majority of owners I talk to, you're operating on a razor-thin margin in terms of your time, your capacity, or both.

## And you're concerned that your profits will continue to erode the more you grow.

What happens if you get sick and you're out for a month or more? That might have been a distant worry until we all experienced 2020 and the pandemic. What if you just need a break for a few weeks? Can you leave the business and come back to a business that's not only still there, but has grown and brought on great new clients while you were gone?

These are serious and important things to think about. The question is, are you ready to take the courageous actions to build a service business that scales… that exists to serve you, and support your lifestyle?

## The Tactic Trap

The way most owners try to escape the '*Entrapment Cycle*™' is by deploying tactics. Maybe it's a new marketing or sales strategy. Maybe it's a new project management tool and approach.

The problem you run into is that tactics just give linear improvements. You'll get growth from many of those tactics, but the fundamental problem will not have changed: everything is still on your shoulders, and you're still the bottleneck.

**The only way forward is to restructure the business so that new growth doesn't hinge on your time and energy.**

This is the key distinction between *Growth and Scale*. Most CEOs use the two words interchangeably. But they are NOT the same at all. Growth is incrementally generating more with the same increase in resources. 2+2 = 4. But if your time is the key resource driving growth, you will quickly hit the ceiling.

If the business only works if you are working in it, do you really have a business? Or do you have a job?

Scale, on the other hand, is much more efficient. It means more *without* the same increase in resources. It means finding unfair advantages to leverage so that you can create more growth with fewer resources. It's using systems to automate repeatable parts of the service to deliver the service more profitably– but doing it in a way where you don't take out what is most special about your brand.

In the next chapter, we'll look at how to break free from the time-for-money challenge by getting the team to execute the vision.

# CHAPTER 3

# My Team Can't Execute My Vision

*"Incredible things in the business world are never made by a single person, but by a team."*
*– Steve Jobs*

Scaling is tough for any business, but it's even more difficult for high-touch custom service businesses. It was true when you were just starting out, but now that you're more established, those obstacles can seem all but insurmountable.

One CEO put it this way:

> *"I'm burned out. I'm spread thin. We're getting terrific client results. The problem is, I feel like I'm personally over-delivering. It's taking too long. I'm too stressed out. I'm having a hard time figuring out who to hire next. I just feel like I'm awash in opportunity, and I'm drowning in stress."*

**A lot of what makes a service business great exists inside of the head of the CEO.**

It's your expertise, hard-won over years of creating exceptional results for your clients. The expertise that was so in demand that you started hiring contractors, and later employees, to help you deliver. Your expertise and the way you interact with clients create that magical experience that your business is built on.

It's your very expertise that's keeping you trapped working in your business. Year after year, growth slows as the work on the desk piles up.

Growth plateaus come as a result of all the demands of keeping your head above water. Two or three years go by with ups and downs in sales, but profits remain stagnant, and the CEO doesn't exactly know why. We see this all the time with firms in the high-six to mid-seven figures in revenue.

It happened to Tom Shapiro of Stratabeat. He saw limitless growth as their services had plenty of demand. But he didn't want his company to take up even more of his time and energy.

Previously, they had expanded. But the quality just wasn't to his standards unless he was very involved.

It just wasn't worth all the stress it created, so he let go of staff who weren't performing. That forced him to work even more in the business.

At this stage, it's common to feel like you can't go forward, and you can't go back, either.

## It's easy to get trapped in your own success

Utilizing the *Scale to Freedom*™ framework, Tom was able to double sales in 7 months after three years of stagnation. But most importantly, he had the freedom to drop everything for a sudden family medical emergency while his team ran his business for nearly a month. During this time, Tom learned he was able to, as he put it, "100% trust my team" to generate amazing results for his clients without him there. His stressful business became "bliss and zen."

This would have been very difficult to do months earlier, and it was life-changing for Tom. That's the power of having a team you can count on to execute your vision.

Fast forward a couple years, and being able to work on his business instead of in it has allowed Tom to increase net profits by 600%. Fast forward another year, and Tom has taken innovation of their service to whole new heights, attracting top-tier clients for multiple 6-figure investments, and they are continuing to increase profits as they scale.

They've also had the space to leverage their cutting-edge SEO processes to write a book, *Rethinking Lead Generation,* that brings quality business in the door. Tom also created a new profit stream with a premium course as a downsell to companies that can't yet afford their services.

The key to making this happen is a refined promise and a common outcome to manage to. With those in place, the team can step up to Tom's high standard of excellence.

Personal emergencies can become giant catalysts to business success because priorities shift, and the CEO is forced to change quickly. But more often, the business was so dependent on the CEO that when the bus hits, the business goes down hard and is never able to really recover.

It's sad to see businesses get knocked out because change came too late. The business becomes a shell of what it was before or has to shut down.

## Most consulting companies are living far below their potential because the team cannot fully execute the vision

Most consulting firms and agencies will never reach their true potential because of it.

Whenever there is a disruption in the team, the CEO gets pulled in. There is so much to react to that time working on the business gets put off.

Many CEOs at this stage look around and find themselves with a team full of very good doers who can get the day-to-day work done.

They do a great job but need more direction. They look to you for answers to questions you know they are capable of solving because they fear making a wrong move.

They are great contributors, but most innovation and new thinking come back to you, the CEO. Every new hire means one more body to take care of. It's an overwhelming amount of pressure.

It takes so much time to train someone to be effective with your processes. It's hard to stay ahead, and you're left picking up the slack while new team members are training. Once they are trained, sometimes you realize they aren't the best fit. Now you're left with a choice to make do or start all over again. Very often, in today's transient workforce, our best staff can move on for their own reasons.

How well can your team execute your vision?:

- Do you feel like your team 'gets' your vision?
- How effectively are they able to execute your vision?
- Do your leaders take on the level of ownership necessary for you to feel confident stepping away?
- Do you find yourself driving priorities to get the right work done on schedule?
- Are you doing a lot of quality control?
- Can you trust your team to handle more growth?
- How confident are you that if you brought on 3-6 new clients this month, your team would be able to handle it?
- Would your onboarding systems hold up? What might break in your fulfillment systems?
- Who would fill in the gaps to ensure clients have a great experience? (This should NOT be your name.)

Based on any gaps you see above, how much money might you be leaving on the table from your team's inability to keep up?

**For many CEOs, that number is millions of dollars.**

Clearly, there is a case for investing in more senior people. But maybe you've done that and still find yourself paying a high salary and being a lot more involved than you hoped to be.

Maybe you don't even have words to describe how you are looking for them to step up. One of the challenges we find is that few CEOs know what is possible for their situation. And still fewer know how to develop their team to seek solutions independently– and execute them without needing your permission for everything. To have more confidence to evaluate and make decisions to move the business forward faster, with less energy from you, and to ultimately execute the vision.

I've been there, and I get it. In my last company, no one else seemed to care as much as I did (even my clients!), and it was frustrating.

## How to attract exceptional leaders who are deeply committed to your vision and client success.

The expansion of your earning potential and wealth is a direct consequence of your ability to get work done through others.

We get the buy-in from others when we create something much bigger than ourselves. Then, we create an opportunity for them and co-create a vision together. That is our secret weapon as visionaries.

As humans, we desire meaningful work. Employees used to be content with a paycheck. Now, you won't be able to retain good people without both a good paycheck and (more importantly) a compelling vision. You must take a stand for and build exceptionalism if you want to attract and retain the best staff. The best employees want to take ownership in a culture of top performers and be a part of the inspiring world they get to help create.

This is the new, beautiful way to grow and scale. Our clients have enjoyed using this secret in their businesses for years. Now, with our changing world, people are waking up and demanding that their work be about *more*. It's a wonderful shift in consciousness that we as employers get to adapt to and benefit from.

This is nothing new. Over a decade ago, groundbreaking research was made popular in Dan Pink's book *Drive: The Surprising Truth About What Motivates Us* and his corresponding TED talk. His research showed that after a certain financial threshold is met, money is no longer a motivator. In fact, he claims it could actually be a *demotivator.*

The top 3 motivators that have nothing to do with money are mastery, autonomy, and purpose. (His fantastic 10-minute animated TED talk is linked on our Hands-Off CEO resource guide: https://handsoffceobook.com/resources.)

**Meaning is now mandatory if you want to attract great people and keep them engaged.**

And that includes you, too!

Meaning will motivate you to scale beyond just the money and personal freedom. Because once we hit a point of success, what we really want is more meaning, more time, and more freedom in our lives.

**Without an inspiring vision, growth will stall. And when challenging times come, we can feel insecure and wonder what it's all for.**

To scale your next-level vision, you likely need more profit. In Chapter 4, we'll look at the top 3 profit pitfalls in a consulting agency and how to move away from linear growth that erodes profit margin.

# CHAPTER 4

# Finding the Profits and Cash to Scale

*"Profit is not something to add on at the end, it is something to plan for in the beginning."*
*– Megan Auman*

Judy felt stuck. Year after year, she worked more hours as the company grew. Even with a decent team, she worked 60 hours per week. Judy was still not creating the growth she knew was possible, and she felt like something was missing.

What was going on was a cycle we call *The Capacity-Growth Trap.*™ She needed *more staff to serve more clients*. But needed *more cash to hire more staff*. But needed *more clients to generate more cash*.

## Capacity - Growth Trap

Need More **TEAM**
to Serve More Clients

Need More **CLIENTS**
to Generate $ Cash

Need More **$ CASH**
to Hire Team

Does this endless loop sound familiar?

It's this challenge where you're weighing opportunities for growth versus the cost of burning through cash reserves. Not certain which role to hire next that will make the biggest difference. Evaluating the ROI for each role you hire to safeguard profits as you grow.

> **The real reason the CEO gets more trapped as the business grows**
>
> The CEO gets more trapped as the business grows because the business can't generate the cash and profits to invest in the resources to grow sustainably. So the CEO is stretched thin filling in the gaps with their own time and energy.
>
> **Cash is needed to scale so you can hire the right people to remove yourself.** Otherwise, you're working more and more in a frenzy to keep up.

But most remedies to solve these challenges just focus on symptoms. *"You need better systems…" "You need better culture…" "Your team needs more training…" "You need more accountability and to get everyone focused on their rocks…" "You need to track better metrics and look at your utilization rate."*

But they are missing the mark and just solving surface-level issues.

A common myth is that installing OKRs, scorecards, core values, and accountability charts.... will solve all your scaling woes.

All the rage are these business operating systems that can *support* scaling by bringing structure. Those who carefully follow the stock scaling advice may have more order, cleaner systems, and staff who are clear on their roles. But those who need it the most don't have time to put the overly complex systems into place. Meanwhile the gap between working in the business and on the business still rages on.

**Because it's an execution framework, not a scaling strategy for their business model.**

The framework won't define what systems and processes will actually grow the company. It's not a strategy to create the cash you'll need to fund scaling. It doesn't show you how to shift the culture in an underperforming team or how to empower your team to move faster without burning out. It just helps you measure and organize accountability, which is incredibly important.

**But without the right scale strategy, you may organize your team to move in the wrong direction.**

You need a strategy to bridge that gap.

Otherwise, the business can feel like a dead-end as you attempt to scale.

CEOs are finding themselves with a successful multi-million dollar company, a growing team, increasing costs, and stress at an all-time high.

They make a nice salary but with more responsibility and stagnant profit growth.

**The Agency Profit Delusion: How much profit do you actually make?**

Profit is a huge blindspot for many agency owners as there seems to be less of it as the company grows. But they reason that it's normal based on the private conversations they have with other agencies.

Most agency owners we talk to are surprised to discover that they're actually not making nearly as much profit as they thought after factoring in the market-level salary they should be paying themselves. Most artificially boost profits on paper by paying themselves less than they'd make elsewhere. But it's not their fault.

The fact is, the whole agency and B2B services market create this dynamic, but you can rise above it.

Most agencies and consultancies exist on weak margins.

Think you're different? Consider how much you take home in salary and draws after all your costs. Now, subtract what your market salary would be for your high-demand skills if you were employed working for another company. The difference is your *actual net profit* in dollars. Calculate your net profit margin based on that.

When you're calculating your real profit margin, you must first subtract how much you'd get paid if you were working somewhere else. What's left is your real profit.

If your business doesn't earn you as the investor at least 20% net profit after replacing you from the other hats you're wearing, you're not making enough compared to the risks you've taken, and your business is at risk.

**Profit is the real problem that keeps CEOs of service firms stuck in the business.**

Our research across hundreds of difficult-to-scale service firms reveals a series of root issues of declining profits.

## Three common profit pitfalls that decimate profits when scaling a service

### Profit Pitfall #1: High Operating Costs

- It's difficult to build repeatable systems to stardardize quality as services and clients are so different.
- High levels of expertise are needed to deliver top-quality work, but highly skilled talent isn't cheap.
- Cash flow is tight due to limited capacity to take on more work. (Making it also harder to afford top people.)

### Profit Pitfall #2: Tight Labor Market

- Fierce competition within a limited pool of available talent.
- Attracting talent sustainably with the rising cost of labor.
- Retaining staff long enough to recoup the investment in training.

### Profit Pitfall #3: Competitive Pricing Pressure

- Overreliance on referrals and fear that charging too much will lead to fewer sales.
- Client resistance to paying what it costs to deliver the service.
- It's hard to stand out even though your services are 10X better than the competition.

At the core, your model is chronically unsustainable because your prices aren't high enough compared to the costs to deliver your services.

The problem is that clients don't care how much it costs you to deliver your services. So how do you increase profits by getting paid what you deserve?

In a consulting agency, this might be easier to impact than you think. When the costs are too high relative to income, there are insufficient profits to adequately staff the firm and deliver a quality service. This can lead to quality declines, profit declines, and/or you have to work more to make up the difference.

But your business is not working with finite numbers. Costs are too high only relative to incoming cash. Grow the right sales, and costs might actually become proportionally quite low.

All that being said, there are simple ways to plug the leaky holes in the bucket to free up cash to invest in growth. For more guidance, read "How to Lower Costs Without Cutting Too Deep" the bonus resources at https://handsoffceobook.com/resources

Cutting costs will free up some short-term cash to invest in creating more long-term profits. But be careful that you don't cut too deep and erode away what generates the most value for clients.

The simplest way to generate more profits, and quickly, is to increase pricing.

**Example 1: 10% increase in fees doubles profits.**

- $100k with 10% profit = $10,000 ; increase fees 10% = $110K
- $10,000 extra profit
- $10,000 original + $10,000 extra profit = $20,000
- Double profits with just a 10% increase in fees!

**Example 2: 50% increase in fees generates 5X profits.**

- $100k with 10% profit = $10,000 ; increase fees 50% = $150K
- $50,000 extra profit
- $10,000 original + $50,000 extra profit = $60,000
- 500% profits increase from a 50% increase in fees!

Please note there may be some additional costs with the second option, but many of our clients see minimal cost increases. These conservative examples demonstrate why those who follow the Hands-Off CEO scaling model report much higher than average net profit margins.

It's why one agency CEO was able to increase net profits by 40% in 9 months. And another was able to increase net profits by 600% over a 3-year period.

CEOs who follow this framework can spend more time working on their business and enjoy the freedom to pursue important activities in their lives besides just working.

## More important than profit is cash flow.

You need more cash coming in than is going out. Many companies fail because they run out of cash. You might think, "Wait, isn't profit most important?" It seems logical, but think for a moment about Amazon.com. They scaled unprofitably for years because they had sufficient cash flow to pay the bills every month.

Strong cash flow builds cash reserves, which protects the business from the inevitable ups and downs. We'd recommend working towards three months of cash. Many will take that to mean to protectively guard cash reserves with their life.

I am instead suggesting is to consciously invest in business growth that helps you accelerate your reserves.

With the right positioning and sales strategy covered in part 2, you can command more favorable payment terms rather than following clients desired payment cycles. Basically becoming their bank as you sit on piles of receivables.

Peter's company would take an average of 90 days to collect invoices. With the right offer, he was able to create new terms, and now invoices are paid on average in 9 days.

Peter shared that a few clients kicked and screamed at first, then got over it. In a matter of a couple weeks, they had $300,000 of extra cash on hand to hire needed staff and built a war chest to weather up and downs.

**Accelerating cash flow gives you the resources to invest in growth today.**

In a perfect world, get paid up front for every engagement. That should be your goal.

The better way to scale (and increase net profit by up to 600%):

- Solve more expensive problems for clients who will invest more for proven results and certainty.
- Focus sales offers on results allowing you to command much higher price points with less price resistance. Offer valuable outcomes (not deliverables).
- Higher fees mean you can double or more the gross profit margin, generating the cash to sustainably hire good people to run the day-to-day operations.
- Train operations leaders to operationalize the new, more valuable offer, innovate systems to scale, and build capacity within the team.
- The above foundation frees the CEO to focus on new, lucrative opportunities and innovations. Increasing profits by working less in the business.

Making the right sales to the right clients means that profits and cash flow increase as you scale.

Later in part 2, we'll talk about how to solve BIGGER problems, create incredible outcomes, and become an indepensable growth partner for your best clients.

In the next chapter, we'll look at which growth stage you're in and exactly what you need to do to progress to your next level of success.

# CHAPTER 5

# Growth Stages as You Scale Up

*"Growing too fast isn't the problem - it's more often you're growing too slow."*

There are growth stages that consulting agencies get stuck in as they grow.

I've personally observed these growth stages across 14 years of my business career consulting with hundreds of CEOs in a wide variety of business services and consulting companies. A unique and common constraint is finding talent to replace the brilliant CEO that clients often expect to be hands-on in their projects.

Included are estimated gross revenue numbers, but take them with a massive grain of salt. It varies depending on a number of factors, including pass-through revenue (cost of goods sold) and the average value of a client.

> IMPORTANT: Pay most attention to the symptoms of each stage, even if your income range is well past it. When symptoms persist into later stages, often an earlier step was missed.

It can become a persistent (and expensive) thorn in your side that is holding you back from your next stage.

**For maximum impact, I invite you to read this from a place of 'I know nothing,' the mindset where incredible breakthroughs begin.**

| "Start-Up" | "Pit of Death" | "Mid-6 Figure Stall" | "7-Figure Slump" | "I'm Still Driving Everything!" | "Growing Your Legacy |
|---|---|---|---|---|---|
| $0-250k | $250-500k | $500K-$1M | $1-3M | $3-5M | $5-10M |

## "Start-Up" ($0-$20k/mo)

*"What are we doing? What am I selling?*
*How do I sell it?"*

You get a bit of traction. Then…

*"Oh, look, a squirrel!"*

Your entire business model (if you can call it that) is trading time for money, and you're working really, *really* hard. You're just trying to figure out what you are doing and what will work.

You start to build a reputation for great client successes. That brings more referrals and word of mouth.

Any work = good work.

Things are just getting off the ground, and you pride yourself on being custom and high touch. Clients are 100% buying you, your skills, and your time.

**To graduate from this level:**

The business owner starts to hire contractors to lend a hand and free up more hours for a bit more growth. *Shortcut:* Deliver excellent work and dramatically increase revenue per client by focusing on results.

## "Pit of Death" (Commonly stuck between $20-40k/mo)

*"Every day I'm hustlin'"*

This stage really sucks! It's hustle city. You're likely continuing to take on any work that comes in, and it's all on you to make sure results happen.

You have created a very stressful job where you work too much and aren't making enough money to justify it. More than likely, after expenses, you could get paid a lot more in a corporate job (maybe a past job that you hated).

You've never had more demands on your time. Your spouse may be very frustrated at the long hours you work and important family events you missed. Many at this stage fear not having enough time with their kids as they grow, and other important relationships suffer.

After days spent firefighting, you may wonder if it's worth it.

It feels risky– because it is! Burnout is common here. Many at this stage will either end up taking a lot less home, or they are working crazy hours– 80-120 hours per week is not uncommon.

Everything moves forward through your own sheer will.

> NOTE: Founders here can be very stubborn and unsuccessfully try the same thing over and over. Being indecisive can also be a challenge that can keep them stuck here. Rather than trusting themselves and taking decisive action aligned with a compelling vision, they may be overly influenced by staff, non-owner spouses, and advice from mainstream books, etc. that oversimplify service scaling.

What they don't know is that they haven't yet committed fully to scaling. They want it, but they aren't "all in" yet. When they finally commit, things will change.

A big decision is needed: stay small and cut back, or make the leap to go all in. It can feel terrifying. A massive mindset shift is required to initiate that next step of investing ahead in the company.

At this stage, the right mentor can help you blast past this roadblock very quickly.

Many companies will close their doors at this stage because the owner doesn't want to continue on. She is offered an opportunity too good to pass up and is just so burned out that she has to take it. (This is also a great place to recruit top talent who realize they don't want the demands of being a business owner.)

> **To graduate from this level:**
>
> At this point, the CEO gets a little more focused. He makes a conscious decision to grow past this stage and starts to see the value of hiring more doers to get the work done.

## "Mid-Six Figure Stall" (stuck between $40-90k/mo)

> *"Growth is painful. Change is painful. But nothing is as painful as staying stuck where you do not belong."*
> *– N. R. Narayana Murthy*

The real problem at this stage is that the business is not profitable or sustainable enough to scale. So you have to make up the difference by working more or your income suffers.

More growth has happened. But now, imagine all that mess in the "Pit of Death" x2. Many of those same symptoms follow you here, which is why you want to move through this phase quickly. You are in growth mode (not scaling), which means more of you. But it's a relief to be able to afford more dedicated staff as you are offloading more menial tasks.

Projects are still very custom. A prospect comes to you with a problem, and you have a solution. It's always custom, and it relies heavily on you as the CEO to be the lead strategist and to ensure quality control. You see incredible client wins, your reputation grows, and more referrals come your way.

You would like more of the right type of clients, but you are just too busy to spend much time prospecting.

You delegate more tasks, likely relying on a lot of independent contractors who are fitting in your business between all their other clients. As you delegate more tasks, it's like you have more people to babysit and more hands tugging at you.

You are wearing a dizzying amount of hats, playing CEO, project manager, client success manager, CFO, marketing, sales... and on and on. The team you can afford are doers but not leaders. Or maybe you have a great leader that is just part-time and cannot give you their full-time attention.

You have to crack the whip to move projects and initiatives forward. Meanwhile, you're trying to figure out all the systems you need to get past this stage.

With higher commitment and more resources, this is in some ways, a simpler stage than others. Many at this stage are so determined to become a million-dollar-per-year company that they seek out help to get there as quickly as possible.

**To graduate from this level:**

FOCUS! Stop taking on clients that aren't a good fit. Expand your price points and go after profit-sweet-spot clients with a laser focus.

At this point, the CEO may wise up and realize that he/she may not be the best person to be managing and driving forward client projects, which frees up the capacity to sell and deliver more work.

## "7-Figure Profit Slump"... Got past $1MM, and I'm the bottleneck to more growth! ($90k-250K/mo)

*"In a competitive world, adversity is your ally.*
*The harder it gets, the better chance you have of insulating*
*yourself from the competition."*
*– Seth Godin*

For some, progressing to this stage is amazing because it's likely a huge load off. You're in less of the minutiae. You have less on your shoulders as you have more skilled people on your team.

Lots of consulting agencies get stuck in the low seven figures. The complexity has grown and there are more clients, but not all of them are the *right clients*. Some clients were accepted out of necessity to keep the doors open. Legacy clients may be at lower fees as the business grows around them.

Every time the business grows, the systems are stressed and need major updates. Speed to implementation is often slow due to siloed work and the team being undertrained with an unclear vision to follow. Accountability structures can be weak, which makes the CEO feel they have to be very involved because the team isn't taking enough ownership. Unless there is solid management in place, it all comes back to the CEO.

You are still the hunter, the closer, and the lead strategist, and the business relies heavily on you. The pressure can feel crushing at times.

These are the roadblocks that keep the company stuck in the low 7-figures, preventing scale to $5-10 million. In fact, at this stage, many are scared to scale, as they've seen declining profit margins.

**This is a big transition point where you may hesitate to rock the boat, risk more, and work a lot harder to be taking the same or even less home.**

You've seen it go bust for others, and you don't want that to be you. You may have invested upwards of 20 years in your career to get to this point, and it can be scary to shake things up. Just like at earlier stages, you know that new skills are needed for both you and the team.

**To graduate from this level:**

FOCUS even more!! One standardized, compelling, and replicable offer that can be operationalized, led, and delivered by the team.

Profit becomes a huge focus! Your time must be shifted to working on the business and leading growth. Expand the vision and reposition the company to attract the highest quality clients who will pay a lot more.

As you increase profits with better quality clients, fire lower-end clients. Clone strategic roles so quality increases without you working with every client. Standardize your sales process to acquire clients more systematically. When appropriate, hire and train sales strategists to take the pressure off you to be free to focus on the highest value growth opportunities.

## $3-5M+ Why am I Still Driving Everything!?!

Here, the demands can compound if your leaders can't level up with growth.

Todd, who owns a successful high 7-figure consulting company, put it this way…

*"I want to be functioning more in the CEO role. But now that we've grown, I'm having to be involved in all that again. I am spending chunks of my day on tasks I don't feel comfortable handing off to anybody on my team right now. It was fine when we were smaller, but I'm now pulled back into everything, and I feel like the business is getting a little out of control."*

At this stage, you have a good team in place. You have managers who have helped you get to where you are now. But they may not be the leaders who can take you to the next level.

**From a $10-million agency CEO:**

"The $3-million level just kicked my ass. We were stagnant, and it was so brutal. To get through it, I had to upgrade my management team. *That was the hardest stage because I took too long to upgrade the managers.*

It took me a year before I had the courage to tell my managers, "You're not cutting it, and I need you to go despite you being amazing and loyal to me for the last couple of years." It was actually just admitting that to myself. And then the other part is really making a decision that it's the right thing for the business.

The needs of the many outweigh the needs of the few. Sometimes, you have to make personal sacrifices because the needs of the business and the families that I've got here outweighed that personal sacrifice I had to make to protect everybody here.

You've got to think of a business as its own person. It's an entity. So you have to make decisions in the best interest of the entity that puts food on your table and your employees' tables. It's what helps your customers and all the vendors that you work with."

– Shawn Buck, CEO of Newsletter Pro

Philip Nickerson described it as letting go of being involved in every project and overcoming the need to check up on things every day, which is a considerable shift, as most of their projects are worth several hundred thousand dollars or higher.

It's being patient with the learning curve as he trusts his team and his capable operations leader. He says it's "head shifting" that comes up over and over. What's interesting is that Philip, who is a very analytical engineer, now shares that that mindset was the biggest thing that got him to this stage.

**To graduate from this level:**

Assess if you have the right leaders for where you are going. You need advanced leaders who can own their own departments. Leaders who can lead, execute, and envision better ways to drive growth from their key areas of the business. Once you have the right leaders, *you need to let go.*

## $5-10M+ Growing Your Legacy and Staying Humble

At this stage, your model must scale beyond you. You need to have the foundations set in the earlier stages to scale sustainably and profitably.

Your ability to see clearly and make sound decisions is very important.

Micheal Palma, an agency talent match expert, has observed this pattern over the past 33 years,

*"Agencies die from $5-10M because the CEO can't say no. The inability to say no to the big office space, to the RFPs, or to that prestigious new account. The new business sounds great, but how are the margins? How does it impact team morale? Too often, agency owners lose the account, and then the big space [or other lavish expenses] chokes them.*

*It's hard to stay humble when you go from 5 million to 10 million, and now you have holding companies talking to you about buying your business. The money changes you. My key advice is to stay humble. Create an environment and establish a winning culture of respect and humility."*

Dennis Conforto, who went from being a homeless teenager to founding several $100-500 million dollar companies, had this to say about how to get people in a company dedicated to growth at this stage and beyond:

*"Don't be threatened by allowing other people to be equal in the business. Surround yourself with humble, coachable people who can define what success looks like.*

*Focus on coaching people who are responsible for growing and protecting the brand. The brand must be bigger than a person. Your people must understand that a brand is a promise kept. Declare the promise and keep it. Failing to live up to the brand is what makes companies fail.*

*It's counterintuitive, but growth is found in adding a zero to the back of the number. If the goal is $1M, add a zero and make it $10M. If it's $5M, add a zero to make it $50M. The difference is a zero. It's just as hard to run a $1M company as it is to run a $600M company."*

Regardless of what number you choose as your goal, the message is clear: think bigger.

**Think A LOT bigger to create more opportunities for others within the brand and leave behind old ways of thinking.**

Jim Padilla from the Opportunity Makers Podcast, who is the CEO of a successful growth agency, summed up scaling in this way:

*"We get so stuck in doing the things that brought us here. Evolving past this place usually means some form of letting go of it. And that's terrifying to most people.*

*Scaling past it is all about clarity of vision and purpose. If I know what the end objective is, then we just bring in the right people, the process, the system, and the team to make it happen.*

***It is not that I have to change it. It's that I have to create the environment for it to be changed.***

*We're creating a brand of people who create a cycle of opportunities for people who create opportunities for people. It's a legacy focused on value. It's creating abundance inside of the opportunity that creates the next opportunity for the person.*

*You have to be able to create something that continues to create. Otherwise, all we're doing is slicing off more and more layers of the pie. That's not just with money, but with time, effort, energy, and credit.*

**You're going from a place where you're literally scaling by your effort versus scaling by impact that creates greater growth within the model."**

To sum up our findings which are relevant to all stages:

1) Stay humble and hire humble, coachable people.
2) Build your company by creating an environment and culture to deliver your brand promise.
3) Create opportunities for others by thinking A LOT bigger and sharing the credit and rewards.

## Which stage do you most relate to?

Are there any symptoms from an earlier stage that still happen often in your company? Where have you fallen back into past stages? When you experience more growth? When you lose a key staff member? Or is there some other trigger?

Remember to look at the symptoms of each stage more than the gross revenues. If you find your income level much higher than the stage where you are, there is a lot of opportunity for positive change.

A big misconception we see many make as they attempt to graduate through these stages is to believe they need to sacrifice client value and results for scalability.

This typical approach risks turning a consulting agency into a cookie-cutter commodity that erodes market position and reputation, along with the fees you can command. All this can lead the CEO to burnout as you work harder to make up for weak value in the model.

## The right kind of growth is like a series of dominos.

Sustainable growth is team-driven growth. It requires a more expansive vision to be a world-class leader in your space. It requires focus to attract the right kind of clients and scale the right types of offers that allow you to charge 2X to 10X higher fees than your competitors. It will give you the profit and funnel the cash flow that's critical to continue to stay ahead of costs and further invest in growth.

It will also allow you to profitably attract and retain top talent to fulfill your brand promise and lead your industry. But to be world-class, you've got to choose what you'll be world-class in.

As you reposition your business to elevate results, cash flow, and profitability, you will focus your team in the right direction with your high energy, passion, and clear vision forward.

The series of dominos start with the right foundation. Next chapter, we will look at four common service models, including one that can scale to $10 million and another with an infinite scale beyond $10 million.

# PART 2

The Foundation for Scale

# CHAPTER 6

# Four Ways to Scale Your Service Firm - Service Product Positioning Matrix

We talked previously about the real reason so many CEOs stay stuck working in the business. Each new increment of growth further traps the CEO because he or she hasn't created a team and culture that takes ownership of outcomes. They are great helpers and doers, but the CEO is driving everything forward while everyone else waits for direction.

We also identified the key reason that the team can't take ownership: the strategy and service are too custom and cannot be easily replicated. Every client is different because the business is too reliant on referrals rather than a proactive marketing program that attracts its ideal clients.

I am not the first person to point this out.

*"The services in our agency were so custom and hard to manage that we found a way to streamline client delivery. Then our clients complained that our process was so rigid that it was like working with*

*the DMV. We had a lot of churns because clients wondered what they were paying us so much for." - Perplexed Agency Executive*

Mass market scaling systems work by removing variability and customization by selling a set of clearly defined deliverables. This makes it scalable by removing the hardest part to scale: custom strategy.

## The Productized Service Fallacy

The common approach to solve this problem is to "productize." Michael Gerber's iconic book "The E-Myth Revisited" first popularized this concept using the analogy of baking pies and assembling McDonald's hamburgers.

I worked at McDonald's for two years in high school and a few desperate months in college. I can tell you that a supersized Big Mac Value Meal delivered by an unskilled worker is a world apart compared to what makes high-value consulting services sellable and impactful.

Positioning your business using this thinking is fine if your services are transactional in nature and you compete on being "reasonably priced." (Whatever that means.) But it's a terrible way to think about positioning high-value, high-impact services.

Assembly line thinking is great once you've defined the positioning, and you're looking at the process level. Gerber is right, you need to systematize your sales, delivery, and finance functions or you won't be able to scale. The problem comes when you think that complete systemization is an end in itself.

It is merely the means to freeing yourself and your team from the repetitive work that must be done so you can focus on the high-value, game-changing work you really get paid to do.

One trapped 7-figure agency CEO put it this way *"If I have to water this down and go down market, and sell lower-end services, it's just not worth it."*

Our CEOs are relieved to find that there is another way to scale that doesn't require them to lose the competitive spark that makes their business special.

It means they don't have to strip out the custom strategy that creates the amazing client results that define their brand. It means they can make their high-touch spun gold service highly profitable, sustainable, and scalable. (See Quadrant 4 below.)

## Service sustainability issues are rooted in the incorrect assumption that value comes from a process or deliverables.

**But processes and deliverables don't equal results.**

The results can vary dramatically so lower certainty in your ability to define a bigger outcome = price resistance, longer sales cycles, and low sales conversions. These challenges can be offset by the trust transferred in a referral and by the charisma of the founder, but are those really scalable?

Be very careful to observe the unintended consequences of business models focused on process and efficiency. They rarely can account for the deeper connection between sales and scalability.

Trust your instincts. Be careful with advice that comes from well-meaning operations strategists who don't understand your clients (and often have a lot less sales experience than you).

Companies struggle with stagnation when clear value isn't baked into the service offer because prospects aren't inspired to take action. They may be very efficient but are overly reliant on referrals because their offer isn't sexy enough to cut through the noise, making business aquisition harder than it needs to be.

## There is a better way.

Instead of diluting your offer and client results with a commoditized offer, you can *elevate* results as you increase sustainable profits as you scale. Let's look at four different scaling models in the *"Service Product Positioning Matrix."*

## VALUE VS. SCALABILITY

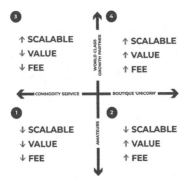

## Service Product Positioning Matrix

### 1 - Amateurs

Low skill and expertise and are easy to replicate. Can be offshored or automated for cheaper.

NOTE: These service providers fill the market with noise and tend to erode buyer confidence throughout the industry.

### 2 - Boutique 'Unicorn'

Exceptional results. Value seen in expertise of top leaders, especially the founder.

CEO's connections and charisma drive growth, making it common for the CEO to be pulled into delivery.

Broad market focus can mean some clients get a lot better results than others. Cash flow gaps are often filled with lower-quality clients that eat up capacity for growth. These offers tend to be focused on deliverables rather than results because that's how it's always been done.

Leadership may recognize they are underpriced for the results they deliver. But clients may give pushback on paying higher investments than their competitors charge. Small, resource-demanding ramp-up projects involving the CEO are the norm to build trust. The CEO is often needed to upsell into bigger commitments, which creates growth bottlenecks.

## 3 - Scalable Commodity Service

Most common model taught to scale services. Customization and variability have been removed as much as possible to package into standardized deliverables. Easy to replicate or offshore for cheaper, so susceptible to market fluctuations. Intense pricing pressures make the model easily commoditized.

High cost of infrastructure and systems to deliver profitably at scale, which sometimes requires rounds of equity funding. Razor-thin margins, so clients must be acquired at a low cost.

Lucrative if you can manage thin margins with cost advantages like cheap labor and custom software automation.

## 4 - World Class Growth Partner

More scalable as it's focused on one client, one problem, and one outcome. 80% Automated by systems and processes. <20% Customization within a proven framework. Sustainable growth positioned as a boutique growth partner. Builds strong cash flow and wealth.

Very high perceived value and quality increases as you scale.

Sustainable and infinite fee growth relative to value.

Can pay a lot to acquire a client, making sales and self-funding growth much easier!

Great model for small-to-medium-sized consultancies and agencies. Can be used as a cash cow to spin off other businesses from unmet market needs related to your service. Many of our clients use this sustainable model to build a *'Hands-Off CEO Ecosystem'* that funds even more expansive businesses, as outlined below.

BONUS - Next Level:

Tech Enabled Services - $10 million +

I debated including this gem, as we want our clients to have have an advantage of being ahead of market adoption. This next level is the Holy Grail, only accessible with a high degree of mastery. This model can scale as big as there is market demand.

Automating parts of your proven framework in Quadrant 4 with proprietary software can replace the 'human automation' parts of service. You retain the exact positioning that was successful to this point and enjoy insane margins (50-80%) that you can pass on to the client, or keep with high-end brand positioning.

You could also spin off the software into a separate brand that is self-serve for a wider market that has the potential to scale to $100-200MM. With the rapid advances in software and AI, the barriers to entry have never been lower. You have an advantage over other technology solutions because you are standardizing the best practices that you've proven in your agency work (paid R&D).

**This is the wave of the future and is a massive area of opportunity for those early to market before software-driven, tech-enabled services become commonplace!**

This model generates incredible profits as it automates boutique-level innovation. This is a SCALE strategy appropriate at mid-7-to-8 figures. Founders I know who've added proprietary technology to automate parts of service delivery increased their EBITDA multiple over three times their industry average, adding millions of dollars to the value of their company.

This is little talked about because the founders sign NDA agreements when they sell, keeping all these juicy details under lock and key.

## Which quadrant of the *Service Product Positioning Matrix* most resonates with you?

Looking over each quadrant, what do you notice? The prevailing scalability models require you to take steps backward! Moving from Quadrant 3 down to Quadrant 2 results in a drop in value, a drop in client outcomes, and a drop in price you can command.

**The grass is not always greener on the other side. You just have new problems to solve.**

I'd deal with capacity issues over profitability and product *sellability* issues any day of the week. Be careful what problems you are trading because it just might make things worse!

Do you really want to go backward from all the years you've spent fine-tuning what it takes to deliver exceptional client outcomes? NO!

ALL exceptional service companies grapple with this problem. They don't know what to do as the tradeoffs are considerable, and they don't see a better way. They can't move forward, and they can't move back.

That is, until now.

Let's leave this mass-market advice to the less sophisticated providers in your industry and those who don't have the chops to deliver the high-level results that you can.

**What we need to do is find a way to make your greatness scale!**

In the next chapter, we will outline how to create an "Irresistible Offer" that can be compelling in any economy and will enable you to dramatically increase profitability aligned with the superior outcomes you already provide for your clients.

# CHAPTER 7

# Bold Actions Create Bold Growth

*"Conformity is the jailer of freedom and
the enemy of growth."*
*– John F. Kennedy*

I've heard from hundreds of consulting agency CEOs who want to have a flow of their most ideal clients coming in but are not sure what to do next. They have limited time to focus on growth because they are too involved in the day-to-day of the business. So they try to delegate sales to perhaps a savvy account manager or a salesperson they hired who has a great resume.

They invest months training a salesperson who makes a few small sales, but most sales are dependent on their own time and existing network.

*"What is really working is referrals, but there is not enough
to reach our growth goals. I've tried hiring salespeople, but it
only generated a couple of tiny projects,
which I closed myself."*
*– Frustrated CEO*

What this also means is that every client that comes in the door is different, which means to get results, the CEO has to be very involved. First with creating a totally custom package. Then a tedious custom proposal. Then clients are trained to expect you there and will insist on your ongoing project involvement, or they'll cancel.

When less ideal work comes along, maybe you need the cash flow, so you take the work. And it traps you more in the business, with even less time to create intentional growth.

Trevor and Jennifer were trapped in this cycle. They actually enjoyed having a large variety of clients, but their team couldn't work independently. Meanwhile, Trevor had no time to grow the business, and the owners were working 70 hours per week. The firm needed more clients to hire the staff needed to free up the owners.

They wanted their business to be an asset they could sell one day. And in the meantime, escape the cold Canadian winters to live in Costa Rica for two months out of the year.

He attended one of our live events where he learned about repositioning the firm to attract world-class clients who would pay a lot more. He could see the approach could give him what he wanted, but he was hesitant.

*"If we focused on a particular vertical, we won't be able to work with a lot of different types of clients, which I really enjoy."*

I said, *"Well, can I ask you, Trevor, do you enjoy working 70 hours per week?"*

*"No, I don't enjoy that."*

*"Do you enjoy not being able to have five weeks of vacation? Do you enjoy not having a company that you can sell as an asset someday?"*

*"No, I don't enjoy that."*

I continued, *"To get where few owners ever get, you have to be willing to do things that other owners aren't willing to do. What we're talking about is a sustainable path to owning a business that serves your dreams. To build a business that will enable you to go to Costa Rica for five weeks and come back to a growing company with everything humming along smoothly.*

*That doesn't mean you'll never bring on these other types of clients. In fact, getting out of the day-to-day means that you can actually enjoy obscure pet projects because now you have the time and space to scratch that itch."*

This made perfect sense to Trevor. Going through the process, they even found a niche that had enough focus to streamline their business, with enough variety to keep their team stimulated.

To create a more expansive future, you've got to be willing to let go of what's causing the current challenges.

You've got to be willing to move past approaches that may have worked to get you where you are now but no longer serve your goals.

Foundational to that is repositioning your business to be a world-class growth partner with your clients. Offering deliverables alone just won't cut it. Your best clients want more.

**6 Reasons why most CEOs will not take this bold position...**

1. They are more committed to feeling "safe" continuing the path that got them here rather than creating the results they desire.
2. They are afraid they can't consistently deliver tangible results because their focus historically hasn't been on outcomes.
3. They're afraid they'll look bad to the rest of their industry by going against the grain.
4. They are too busy working in their business.
5. They are timid taking calculated risks to generate very high rewards.
6. They may care most about removing themselves as far away from clients as possible because the company has become a ball and chain they resent.

**To generate the cash to scale, you get to define exactly who you will be world-class for, what high-level problems you want to solve, and what outcomes you can provide under the most ideal circumstances.**

That's what allows you to own a market by standardizing 80% to 90% and identifying the remaining 10% to 20% of the service to customize. This allows you to deliver boutique-level results, with premium pricing, but in a scalable and profitable way.

An example of this is Mark Arnold. His firm was already world-class in the small banking and credit union industry as the leading branding and marketing expert.

But when we connected with Mark, he'd packed so much into each day that he was about to fall over.

His business would bring in sales, but they were smaller projects that created inconsistent cash flow, requiring more of Mark. He was booked solid and wanted more team-led growth. But, unfortunately, clients always wanted *him*.

Mark wanted long-term commitments from clients so that he didn't have to personally upsell clients each time. This would also give him certainty to invest in more growth.

Right as the pandemic hit, small banks freaked out and slowed investments.

When we put together his Irresistible Offer for a $100k package, Mark was nervous that clients wouldn't buy it. Mark put faith in the proven process and went from selling mostly $10,000 to $30,000 projects to selling $100,000 to $120,000+ growth programs.

His visual *Client Success Map* acts as a powerful sales tool that makes selling so much easier. It's the foundation for all their marketing and has enabled them to increase fees by 600%.

Mark found that clients liked seeing the bigger picture and wanted more certainty. While his clients were cutting budgets everywhere else, they more than tripled their investment with Mark's firm because they now had a vision of an elevated growth path with outcomes that they eagerly desired.

Mark has dramatically cut the amount of time he spends on each client engagement. Longer engagements were the key that increased cash to scale and unlocked more growth for the business and freedom for Mark.

He's also been shocked to realize that both quality and net profits have grown as they've scaled their successful firm— which was the exact opposite of what Mark expected.

**Like Mark, many trusted market leaders are NOT fully monetizing their expertise.**

Many are vastly under-earning for their skills and years of experience because their offers don't have enough focus.

Instead, let's leverage your solid track record of results to attract the very best quality clients who will gladly pay more and invest for longer engagements.

Imagine how much easier it will be for your team to operationalize and deliver quality work when they have crystal clarity about who it's for, what they will get, and what success looks like.

Now, they have a clear vision to execute and success criteria to measure against.

Foundationally, that is what you need to scale Excellence, without the CEO doing all the work. In the next chapters, we will break down exactly how to reposition your services to attract your most ideal 'profit-sweet spot' clients. Then how to double or more profits, by commanding significantly higher fees for your services.

# CHAPTER 8

# Your Irresistible Offer

*"It is impossible to progress without change, and those who do not change their minds cannot change anything."*
*– George Bernard Shaw*

**To create efficiencies in your business, you need to focus on the right kind of growth.**

If you haven't first clearly defined what ideal growth is, how do you know what roles you need to most efficiently reach your goals?

**As we introduced in Chapter 6, most consulting business owners never achieve what they really want because they're stuck in a model that doesn't work.**

**The counterintuitive way out is an *Irresistible Offer*.**

Your Irresistible Offer is the secret to unlocking all the freedom you've dreamed about in your business without sacrificing quality or results for your clients. An Irresistible Offer allows you to create a highly profitable and repeatable approach to attract new clients by solving a specific and measurable problem for them.

As shared in past case studies, an Irresistible Offer has allowed our clients to increase fees, and it's the key foundation to scale. It's also the key that unlocked their ability to delegate high-ticket sales as we'll learn about in the next chapter. It's also the reason they do well in spite of ups and downs in the economy because they can stay relevant by tweaking one of the three 'Power of 1s' below that it's built upon.

## Almost every business problem will be lessened by commanding much higher fees.

Yet, few can take this path because they're selling processes and deliverables that clients see as commodities they can easily get from another competitor at a lower price.

The longer you go without creating a sustainable pricing model, the tighter your margins get in terms of real dollars because inflation is always eroding the value of the money you're paid.

The easiest way to become more sustainable for a custom service is to increase your fees. Not just a tiny amount either. The question to ask is…

*"How might I raise my fees by 50 to 100% AND not only keep my best clients but increase their commitment and attract even more ideal clients?"*

The answer is to develop a tangible Irresistible Offer that consistently delivers a valuable reward with certainty at low risk to you and the client.

For most B2B services, the perceived *reward* for the client is low, while the *risk is high*. That's why clients insist on small test engagements, which become bespoke low-profit projects that trap the CEO. What we want to do is jack up the reward and dramatically lower the risk for clients.

**We want to give clients what they want to buy– bolder promises and less risk.**

That's okay if that makes you feel nervous. Nearly all our clients feel this way when they start the process. We walk them through how to do it in a way that's very low risk to the agency. By setting very firm conditions for success, you drive up the client's commitment to your work together so you can *deliver your very best work every time.*

**It's risky only if you can't provide tangible results for clients. This process will *not* work for those without a track record, who aren't true experts or who are delivering little tangible value.**

What clients are coming to you for is a bridge from where they are now to where they want to be. Most clients have a limited vision of what's really possible for their business. How far might you be able to take your best clients across that bridge? In what time span? You get to help them see a bigger, brighter vision of the future than they currently imagine.

# More Certainty = More Income

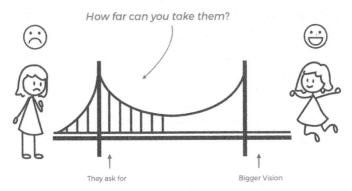

*How far can you take them?*

They ask for

Bigger Vision

How big of a vision could you show them?

**But how can you define that vision when each client is so different?**

For a typical consulting agency, much of the success of a project depends on the client. It depends on their goals. It depends on the budget. It depends on the length of engagement, how cooperative they are, and what they already have in place. It depends on their industry, offer, price, profit margin, sales cycle, collections, processes, marketing, and more.

But what if you got to choose your own factors for success?

Imagine if your business was filled only with exceptional clients. What if your scale strategy was to multiply your most exceptional client wins?

What if you're then only doing focused work with superb clients? How much easier would that be to scale?

## To Attract Clients Who'll Pay Top Dollar For Results Consider...

- Who can we do the most impactful work for?
- What do they already have in place?
- What is the minimum time commitment to do our best work?
- What minimum budget do we need?
- What is the best work that we could do for them?
- How might we generate even bigger results?
- How might we get ideal clients to line up and PAY MORE?

We have a proprietary process we walk our clients through where in four weeks, they have a focused offer that will allow them to scale world-class results. While going through this process, CEOs start to see their work so differently that many will immediately raise rates because they are no longer willing to have their teams work for less. Clients report that limited budgets and project delays can turn into "I'll go find the money. This is our top priority!" Often in a matter of weeks when approached correctly.

Using their new offer, they attract quality clients, retain top staff who want meaningful work, command premium fees, and make competition irrelevant. An Irresistible Offer allows you to fully monetize your brilliance, then deliver that brilliance at scale through your team.

## Why Most Offers Fall Flat

There have been plenty of books written in the last decade about pricing and creating compelling offers. The problem with most of their approaches isn't both valuable and scalable. They usually lack the factor of depth and boldness. Boldness is required to substantially increase prices and drive the profits and cash flow needed to sustainably replace the CEO.

Offers without boldness tend to lack depth, relevance, and specificity. They really aren't sure who that profit-sweet spot client actually is and how to position the services so it's most compelling to them. Most often, when we see bold claims, they don't have an elegant way to back them up. The result is a lot of hot air, and the market has become very wary of big claims that cannot be substantiated.

The problem for most consulting firm leaders isn't coming up with a bold, compelling offer or claim, it's having the internal confidence that they can deliver on it. There's nothing worse than trying to sell something when you doubt you can actually deliver it.

When we work with a firm owner in one of our programs, the cornerstone of creating their Irresistible Offer is to first address the owner's mindset and create an offer that they are 100% confident that the firm can deliver.

We start by digging for gold in your current client results. Then, we work to stretch those results, challenging you to create even bigger results for clients while remaining in integrity with what you can actually deliver.

The key to scaling is generating the right type of growth.

Maybe you are thinking: *"Clients already think we are too expensive… How could I possibly increase our fees? And you want me to double, or even triple our fees?"*

The reality is that you might be perceived as "expensive" for how your business is currently positioned.

**Two 'R's clients use to evaluate what they will pay and when:**

Clients decide the price they'll pay, how deeply they'll engage your services, and how quickly they'll make a decision based on two factors:

1) REWARD - How painful and expensive a problem is to them. This includes the speed and ease with which you can solve it for them.

2) RISK - Their level of certainty that your solution will solve their problem and lead to the outcome they want.

When clients negotiate or ask for small test projects, it's because they don't feel certain. They're speculating, not investing.

To generate strong cash flow and command prices aligned with the value you create, you need to be able to communicate your offer in a way that inspires your clients' supreme confidence. Otherwise, you'll just get the scraps as clients gamble on your services and insist on small projects to "test you out."

## The Power of 1s Formula™:

To scale easily and profitably, you need to know what problem you are solving, for whom, and what you'll actually be delivering. If it's just *"deliverables,"* you can charge at best slightly over market. If you give them tangible outcomes, you can charge a nearly infinite fee based upon the value of the problem you solve for them.

## There are three parts to The Power of 1's Formula™:

**ONE PAINFUL PROBLEM** - we recommend million-dollar problems

**ONE PROFIT SWEET-SPOT CLIENT** - who has access to money and is willing to spend it

**ONE BOLD OUTCOME** - made possible by your work together

It's very difficult to scale a custom services business if you're too wide in any of these areas. Otherwise, there is too much variability in your offers, systems, and delivery to pull off a quality service. It's the kiss of death that makes services mediocre, starting a chain reaction of attracting mediocre clients and a mediocre team.

You need one painful problem to solve for one "profit-sweet spot" client that results in one bold outcome. That's the foundation of an

Irresistible Offer. This approach allows the company to be scalable and allows the team to deliver for clients because the outcome is very clear. The clients can easily see what they're getting because it's quantified and your offer is highly compelling, so it's much easier to sell. Prospects happily sign up and pay premium fees, and commit to longer engagements.

**Get this formula aligned, and your service can sell without a charismatic salesperson. It will sell itself.**

Consider a problem that you actually want to solve and are skilled at solving. I can organize a house, change the oil in a car, or cook a gourmet dinner. But I am not going to be compensated well as they are inexpensive problems that an unlimited number of people can solve well.

### How to Find Million-Dollar Problems to Solve

It's very hard to see for yourself the full impact of your services. Asking clients can help, but how often have clients not realized the full impact of your work? Are there times when you have not gotten credit for exceptional work you delivered? Maybe you have clients who don't share that information. What if your past clients aren't actually where you can deliver the biggest impact?

That million dollar problem could be the same problem for a client with deeper pockets. It could be seeing a breakthrough innovation in an industry with unmet needs. We help our clients create breakthrough innovation that allows them to stand out from the typical way others operate—and charge A LOT more.

What makes you most frustrated about your industry? How do they get it all wrong? What kinds of outcomes could you create with clients if they doubled down and let you do your best work over the long haul?

Where are your ideal clients underinvesting and missing out on the bulk of profits because they aren't bold enough?

That's where you go.

This takes courage and a different way of thinking to this level of boldness. But it can literally add millions of dollars of growth and transform the course of your business when you get it right.

## A Case Study on Discovering Million-Dollar Problems

Jeff's business was different from many of our other clients. He had a successful surveying consulting company, selling work by the hour. They took the work that came in the door and stayed very busy! In fact, they were already the highest-priced firm in their industry. Jeff didn't see a way to squeeze more out of his pricing model.

When we dug into the business, we discovered that the firm did a lot more than just surveying. They had created a unique process at the intersection of surveying and engineering. Like many of our clients, they were in demand because they had a new approach to an industry problem. Jeff was so close to it that he didn't realize the full value they could deliver or how special they were.

This was a blessing and a curse.

The blessing: what they were doing was so unique that there was no training for it. He had developed unique expertise at a crossroads of two heavily regulated professions.

The curse: profit margins were tight putting high-end professionals into the field to do the work–it wasn't sustainable in his current hourly model. He also couldn't train lesser employees to do the work in a reasonable time or at a reasonable cost.

**Most business owners in this situation can never grow beyond a tiny team.**

As Jeff went through this process, he uncovered that the real value of his process was increasing the profitability of his clients' projects. They were eliminating days of downtime on worksites. When we dug deeper, he realized they were helping clients boost profits by up to 30%! When applied to large development projects, that means big dollars — seven figures of added profits (or more). On top of that, they were helping clients be more productive and greener than any of their competitors.

Once they realized the impact they were making, they immediately increased prices by 20%. That adds tremendous profit growth to the firm every year.

They also gained the confidence to stop all work for slow-paying clients, no longer needing to offer payment terms. This allowed them to accelerate cash flow and collect on $300,000 of outstanding receivables in a matter of weeks. They used the cash to invest in the staff they needed to grow.

Jeff had so much more in him, so we pushed him to think deeper to get off the hourly treadmill.

It was challenging for him to see outside the "industry box." Most industries have a common way of doing things– how you bill, payment terms and even the services you deliver. The opportunity lies just outside of the box.

It was challenging to make these changes, but throughout the process, we helped Jeff see what he was actually selling to clients, summed up in this statement:

*"We double job site productivity and efficiency on large, heavy civil construction projects overnight, unlocking a minimum of $500,000 profit per year."*

How much more might they charge for that? Jeff shared on our podcast that it now means million-dollar contracts.

With that kind of offer, the very top construction companies in the country began seeking them out. They now get to pick and choose top vendors and partners who feed them new business.

His vision for his company grew 20 times overnight. Now all of a sudden, that cushy offer he got for his business the previous year didn't seem like such a good deal. What they do is much bigger than surveying. They are revolutionizing an entire industry, and as a result, they are attracting the best opportunities in the industry.

Your company may be in the habit of saying yes to a lot of work because it paid the bills and kept the lights on. Now, you need to think differently if you want to scale more profitably.

> SIDE NOTE: Most scalability experts advise timidly increasing pricing because they are weak at sales. Just squeeze a few more dollars and cents out of their time-for-money model by being more efficient.
>
> We are all for efficiency but fix your profit model first. You'll see improvement a lot faster.

## Make an Offer They Can't Refuse

Now that you've used The Power of 1s Formula™ to focus your business around one painful problem, one specific type of client, and one bold outcome, it will form the foundation for your Irresistible Offer.

This is the format we start with:

---

*"We create [outcome] for [type of client] [qualifier- time frame, without this painful thing, guarantee, etc.]."*

---

This simple format can be used to brainstorm ideas. Once you have a winner, it will be polished up for presentation. Remember, this is fine-tuned to your specific market and problem. So each business that walks through this process looks very different at the end.

Examples:

"We double job site productivity and efficiency on large, heavy civil construction projects overnight, unlocking a minimum of $500,000 profit per year."

"Grow MRR $500k for enterprise Martech SaaS in 12 months, without increasing cost of acquisition."

"Add at least $100k net profit for manufacturers within 12 Months — all from your existing resources."

"Add $1,000,000 to your food business' revenue in 12-months, without having to beg buyers to put you on their shelves."

"We add $10M of revenue in 3 years for Fashion, Beauty, and Skincare brands without incurring unearned affiliate commission costs."

"We add 6 figures in new net profits in the next 12 months for private practice physicians."

"We increase cash flow $400k in 90 days for CRR providers and add $1M of valuation within 12 months."

"Close enterprise SaaS deals in just six months, without security delays– guaranteed. Save $500k instead of doing it on your own."

Some reading this will say, "It would be nice to see some bold promise examples that are less about money." They miss the point because they are clouded by their old way of thinking.

## Most think tying financial value to services only applies to sales offers, but that's just not true.

These compelling examples above *are from a range of consulting services*– not just sales and marketing.

They include surveying, analytics, software development, finance, M&A, operations, supply chain, and sales and marketing. The whole point is to drill deeper to understand the real impact of the service. To do that, you must know who the profit-sweet-spot client is. In 100% of the cases with our clients, even really exceptional experts with an existing niche were off by at least a couple of degrees.

Why does a couple of degrees matter? Because that can be the difference between long-term commitment and piecemeal custom projects. Two degrees in an offer and positioning can be the difference between an offer accepted at $60k vs. $350k. Really.

It's all about client selection and offering them what they badly want but don't yet know is possible.

## Your biggest blindspot might be that you don't yet know it's possible either.

The key is aligning your services with the right profit-sweet spot client so you can stretch your capabilities. But whatever you do, do NOT make a promise that you aren't willing to keep. Please only use these powerful strategies for good. Sell every service as if your name and integrity are on the line– *because they are.*

Sophisticated buyers won't expect a guarantee if you've nailed their pain points and the outcome they want. This can take some testing, so a way to get faster traction is to explicitly offer a guarantee. But it is not a fit for all cases.

Use the language of your prospect. Aspects they care about that are very specific to how they would say it.

Now that you know *what* to sell, how do you sell a much bigger offer with integrity and confidence? We'll explore the nuts and bolts of this in the next Chapter on How to Sell Bigger Offers and Delegate Sales.

# CHAPTER 9

# How to Sell Bigger Offers and Delegate Sales

## How to sell a much bigger offer with confidence

Top business leaders who are serious about reaching their goals take calculated risks and make safe investments–often ahead of current resources–to reach their goals faster and with more ease.

Ask yourself: *"Is that how I operate?"*

If not, you'll struggle to close bigger sales because you are asking the prospect to do something that is out of alignment with your own beliefs. Value conflicts will stop us in our tracks because, subconsciously, we'll do anything to validate what we see as inner truth, even when it's hurting us.

## Sales is just a transfer of energy and your confidence.

Your job is to *reduce the risk* as much as possible and *increase the reward* so that your consulting services are a safe and lucrative investment. Then, sales resistance evaporates when you are talking to the right person. If you don't see a clear path to results, and if you can't communicate it, then they won't see it either.

To boost your sales confidence, eliminate prospects that would be hard clients to get results for, and only sell to ideal clients!

Yes, that could mean turning away business, but doing so allows you to generate more profit working with fewer clients, which is much easier to scale. (See Chapter 4)

Consider these qualifying questions:

- What questions could you ask that would uncover the amount of success you could have with them?
- What would give you that certainty of result?
- What variables would you need to have control over?
- Who could you *not* work with?
- What do they have in place already for you to build on?
- What resources do they need to allocate to support your work together?
- How would the client need to show up to support the effort?
- What qualifications must they first meet to become a client?

At Hands-Off CEO, we require certain success conditions to exist before we invite clients into our premier flagship Scale to Freedom™ program. There are income requirements. They have to be coachable, willing to show up and do the work, and be a likable leader their team can respect. (We don't ask about all of those things directly, but we have developed a "qualification checklist" that reveals how effective our work will be if they became a client.)

Set your bar high, and see your sales conversations as the client auditioning to be your next biggest case study.

## Who is my profit-sweet-spot client?

If you want to charge more, you must first start by adding more value. It's financially irresponsible for clients to pay you based on your costs to deliver. Frankly, *they don't care what it costs you.*

So our job is to build confidence in your solution for ideal prospective clients.

## Vision Selling to Show a Bigger Vision Forward.

Once you have your Outcome Statement based on The Power of 1's Formula™, how do you sell it for triple or more what most clients are willing to pay?

With a Client Success Map.

Using strategically crafted visuals allows you to invite prospects to see an expansive growth path in front of them. It allows them to "explore" their future within your visual sales map. Your outcomes speak to them, and they begin to sell themselves on why they not only want, but *need* the services you're offering. It's fun to watch… and it makes selling easier.

When we work with a client in our Irresistible Offer Intensive program, we develop their offer together, then our team builds their visual *Client Success Map.* The Client Success Map is a graphic depiction of your Irresistible Offer.

Each of the examples below allowed the company to charge at least double what they charged before while making it dramatically easier to sell. Many consistently sell six-figure and some even sell million-dollar engagements using this tool.

## Client Success Map - *Irresistible Offer*

---

*Your Client Success Map is not a process map.*
*It is an **outcome** map to communicate certainty*
*for your client.*

---

The great thing about Vision Selling is it's not just about sales. If you go and work with a sales expert or advisor, they can help you sell better.

But the problem is that if you're not selling the right thing, it can create a real problem in your business around scalability. So you really need to have a strategy that encompasses marketing, sales, and operations. And that's what the Client Success Map does to make your company more sustainable and scalable.

In the appendix, you can find a larger example of a Client Success Map for our flagship **Scale to Freedom™** program.

**Impacts of Vision Selling**

- Increase price 2x to 4x → Increase gross profit by 100%
- Increase upfront investment from clients → Accelerate cash flow
- Win longer contracts → Deliver bigger client results
- Better case studies → Sales becomes easy to delegate
- Only 'profit-sweet-spot' clients → Your team is hyper-motivated to create client wins
- Simplified delivery → More capacity for growth
- A waitlist of future clients → Peace of mind to invest ahead of growth
- Team-led delivery → You, the CEO, can focus ON growth

This shows the client what they get and when they can expect to get a return on their investment investing for an extended engagement. How long depends on a lot of unique factors, especially the outcome you're delivering. We see a lot between 1-5 years, but a good place to start is 12 months.

**Prospects are already trying to figure out how they'll make back the money they invest in you.**

The Client Success Map allows you to preemptively answer their unasked questions.

This is our secret weapon for selling more clients than you have now, more easily than you've ever sold before, at 50 to 600% premiums.

**MORE CONFIDENCE = BIGGER SALES**

There are certain structural aspects you need to create to sell at much higher prices— all of the things we've just covered. But there's one more thing you need to address. Without it, your Irresistible Offer won't work.

**Confidence.**

If you've not been selling at significant premiums above market averages, you need to increase your confidence to pull it off now. The only real way to do that (and the one way that you can transfer to your sales team) is *greatness*.

When you're great, and I mean really great, at delivering promised client outcomes, it's easy to have supreme confidence when asking for big fees. You know that you can deliver, and you know the client will get a return.

When you hyper-focus on solving one BIG problem, and you know you're good at it, you'll have all the confidence you'll ever need to ask for that big fee.

## A Word About Guarantees

First, you don't need a guarantee, and it's not appropriate in all markets. I've used guarantees to start two different companies and help dozens of consulting companies break into new markets. When done well, it can be a great offer boost.

A few years ago, I wrote a short book titled *Value-Based Pricing Guide*. That little book reveals how to elegantly use guarantees in service businesses. I haven't published it for a few reasons. I've kept the book under lock and key– sharing it with a few outside our private clients– because I knew that the marketing world would pervert it and even use it to do harm.

See, today's typical marketer believes that all you need is a big promise, a couple of outlier case studies, and some (now overused) guarantee language they read about in the latest book on crafting mega-offers.

That misses the point, and the wrong guarantee makes you look amateurish and repels buyers. A bold guarantee will turn off sophisticated buyers if it's not elegantly communicated and backed up– which it rarely is.

The reason to make a big promise– like your Irresistible Offer– and pair it with a guarantee is to demonstrate your confidence in the certainty of the outcome for the client.

**It's not merely a "risk reversal" device. It's a confidence statement.**

Imagine the biggest promise that you can make that you are so confident in, that you could stand by the results for the perfect fit client who meets all the pre-conditions necessary for you to deliver those results.

## 4 Foundations to Scale & Delegate Sales

What does it actually take to effectively delegate premium-level sales? Not just little projects but premium-level packages at a higher-level price point.

1) **You need a standardized Irresistible Offer for a focused client type.** (Are you seeing a pattern here?) This is the foundation you have to have to make this work.

2) **You need to have sustainable pricing to be able to cover your cost of acquisition.** If you can't cover your cost of acquisition, the CEO will always be the one selling it.

3) **You need compelling messaging, documented results, and sales assets to prove the process.** You, as the CEO, can pull all these different results out of your head to prove the process as you're talking to a client, but your sales team can't.

4) **You need sales strategists, not just slick sales guys.** High-pressure "high-ticket closers" are the modern-day used car salesman. Your clients don't want to engage with them, and they won't cut it for the level you want to play. Imagine how effective your sales team could be if they became expert strategists in your proprietary method.

Without the four sales delegation foundations above, it's difficult for even a sales superstar to sell anything of substance.

Vision Selling is how to train sales teams to illuminate an expansive growth path. It's about this bridge from where they are to where they want to be. You are selling the bridge to get to an incredible destination in their business.

Whenever possible, preempt your clients' questions and give them a level of certainty. This supports your team to be experts, and the level of skills required to make a sale is dramatically lower.

Can you see how having these four aspects makes delegating sales significantly easier?

To see how your company measures up, take the *Sales Delegation Readiness Assessment* for your firm: handsoffceo.com/delegate-sales

Now that we've looked at getting your company positioned and structured in a way that it can scale let's talk about how your job as the CEO changes.

# PART 3

## Scaling *Your* Capacity

# CHAPTER 10

# Letting Go of the Superman Complex (A Candid Conversation)

*"There is no limit to the amount of good you can do if you don't care who gets the credit."*

*– Ronald Reagan*

This chapter could be a whole book by itself, so I'll do my best to share the most important parts. The rest of this book deals with more of the tactical parts, but an elevated approach to leading your team makes the difference between leading them to eagerly take ownership to build the business, or just getting a litany of excuses.

Staff will often say that they can't keep up with the pace, there's too much work to do, and appeal for more staff. Proceed Cautiously.

---

*"What happens to so many agencies is they start getting pretty good at getting clients. But then the owner of the business looks around and says, 'I'm working harder than ever, and I'm making less than ever because I'm scaling sideways. I'm adding people to the team, and*

*I'm adding clients, but it's not really taking us anywhere.'"*

*– John Jantsch, Duct Tape Marketing Consultant Network*

---

The reality is that both you and your team will need a new way of thinking to make this transition. That starts with you as the CEO. Without changing your thinking, your vision won't be clearly articulated enough for your leaders to effectively implement it. And even if they are successful in making the necessary changes to the business, the CEO will often sabotage the progress because they don't feel safe letting go.

## The CEO Superman Complex

Consider for a moment Clark Kent. The calm reporter. Always on call, waiting to run into action and save the day—*himself.* What he lacks in experience, he makes up in speed, strength, and brute force.

It feels good for us as CEOs to see a challenge and jump in like Superman to save the day. We are even rewarded with an endorphin rush, releasing addictive chemicals into our bodies that further reinforce the habit.

**It's dangerous when leaders derive significance from the hero's identity. If their identity is tied up in problems to solve they'll create more problems to feel self-worth.**

How is being the smartest person in the room keeping you stuck in perpetual fix-it mode? How might this be stifling the brilliance of your team? What opens up for the business when you release the emotional need to be *needed?*

Every time we rush in to save the day, we send the message to our teams that we do not trust them to make decisions without us. Just like Superman, an ongoing circumstance is created where you're reactive, always needed. It creates learned helplessness in your team where work is bottlenecked by you.

As Jamie Birch, a Scale to Freedom alumni, shared "Put away the cape, and stop carrying around the heavy phone booth." Empower your skilled team to do the work and make decisions independently. Then, you can become more *hands-on* in the areas of our businesses that most need your skills now.

## Become the Wise Yoda.

Another Scale to Freedom alumni, Jason "Wally" Waldron, chose Yoda as the leader to model after. Yoda is deliberate and intentional. He asks questions. He sets the bar high, gives guidance, and goes into his cave and is not needed all the time. Though it feels like a slower approach, it develops within the Jedi the independent skills, confidence, and mindset to overcome immense challenges and go on to win the war for the galaxy. Without Yoda. And to even carry on Yoda's legacy after he is gone.

Yoda didn't emotionally need the glory of the battle won. But he celebrated the victory (even if just in hologram).

We can learn from Yoda to find our significance outside of being the doer in our business.

Yoda-like leaders develop within their team a deeper understanding so they are able to do it on their own.

## Your role and how you add value to the company changes as the company grows.

It's critical that you understand and think about how your role evolves as the company grows. Without this awareness, we remain stuck in old patterns that no longer serve us.

Growing your company to where it is now required a lot of your own hard work and effort. It may have felt grinding at times. But you no longer need to work harder to get ahead. Working harder and *doing* more at this stage is counterproductive and will actually keep you stuck in the business, stalling growth.

Be aware of the mind virus where working harder makes you feel safe and in control.

At each new level of growth, it's easy to fall back into these comfortable, deeply worn ruts that have proven to work in the past. On an unconscious level, we'll take all-consuming stress over the fear of losing control of what we've worked so hard to build. Damaging your hard-earned reputation or letting clients down are just not options.

## Next-level productivity as a CEO is no longer about doing more

*The key to scaling is getting more done—through other people.*
*Through efficiencies not tied to your own time.*

That requires safely letting go! Some things need to shift in order to reach the next level without negatively impacting your business or your life.

There are some incredibly disciplined CEOs who become productivity masters. They can squeeze more in a day than five ordinary people. I used to compare myself to these top producers and felt that I'd never measure up consistently. Sure, I could produce superhuman output in bursts. But not in the daily consistent way they were able to.

I saw productivity and growth as me becoming increasingly more efficient, transitioning from task to task to do more. As a creative person, forcing that on myself was a pressure that was pure misery. It drained my energy, and on those days, my soul felt like it was rotting.

While personal discipline is important, that doesn't mean driving growth through sheer willpower. A better place to apply discipline is in taking care of your mind, body, and spirit so that you can be at peak physical and mental performance to lead a company. That means feeding your mind to become a better leader. It means developing internal mastery by paying attention to nurturing personal relationships, exercise, quality sleep, spiritual practices, nourishing foods, and meditation.

Less mature leaders think they don't have time for this. At the same time, they are stressed, unfulfilled, and experience strain in their personal relationships. As Steven R. Covey famously stated, *"Put first things first."* That means proactively caring for your personal relationships, your physical health, and your mental and spiritual well-being.

Otherwise, you'll be constantly reacting to fires because *your life is on fire*. I say that lovingly, knowing what it's like to be an unbalanced entrepreneur who created a dumpster fire in my own life.

There is a big difference between being a productive producer and leading productivity in a company. They are different skills.

I felt such relief when I learned that. No longer did I need to work a "normal" work week like everyone else. I didn't need to keep an overpacked schedule of long hours to keep up. My work became aligned with my dream life, not an average existence. If you're like me, you started your own business because you desired an exceptional life full of meaning and freedom.

Now, you can have that, too.

Getting this alignment reignited a yearning for the next level. A new drive that can otherwise fizzle after hitting key financial milestones, wondering if it's worth it to rock the boat.

From analyzing hundreds of CEOs and how they get work done in their business, productive producer CEOs tend to have the hardest time letting go at their next stage of growth. They actually have more stress because they have a growing team to manage, plus all the work they feel they must personally do.

Without a shift to move into a more mature style of productivity, you become a machine and a slave to a never-ending to-do list. And growth will stagnate.

## The 'Lifestyle Business' Lie

Many will hesitate to grow, reasoning that they just want a "lifestyle business."

See if you can find any holes in this logic.

*Lifestyle business = do more of the work so I can have control = less staff to manage = more freedom.*

Make sense?

**Please stop dimming your dreams and calling it a "lifestyle business."**

What most people think of as a "lifestyle business" does NOT give them more freedom. It gives them a sense of control. But it's a time-for-money trap driven by the CEO's time and personal energy.

Otherwise known as…a job.

> "I thought in the beginning that what I really wanted was this lifestyle business where I could make 100 thousand bucks a year and just coast through life. The reason I thought that was not because I actually wanted that but because I wasn't having the success I wanted. So I made myself feel better

> by telling myself I owned a lifestyle business and that all the challenges I wasn't willing to face were okay for me not to face because this is a lifestyle business. That's what it's designed to be, right? It was just not true. I was lying to myself."
>
> – Shaun Buck, $10M+ Agency, CEO of The Newsletter Pro

Many still operate this way with a growing team, and it just means an extra job of managing people but still needing to control everything.

What's missing is a strategy to increase the CEO's productivity by developing the ability to find good people and develop them. The trick is freeing your time to do that and getting the business model to support it.

Not everyone wants to do this. That's okay. But let's call it like it is: what most refer to as a lifestyle business is really a stressful job with several bosses. Flexibility, but no freedom, and every vacation is a working holiday. Fun!

## What a *real* lifestyle business looks like...

Brandon had intended to keep his software consultancy small to maximize his income. Their exceptional services had ballooned quickly, driven by his own hard work. His small team, he couldn't keep up, and he made up for it by working daily until 1 am (sometimes through the night).

His 'lifestyle' business was eating him alive, he was missing out on key moments with his kids, and his wife was frustrated. Yet, he didn't know what else to do because he had to support his family.

We first helped him cut 20 to 30 hours off his work week. A few months later, he had a reasonable work week. Then, we helped him streamline operations and cut onboarding costs by 67%. Then, he doubled his fees, which gave him the profit and cash to hire both a manager and a senior-level developer to take over running the business. Within 18 months, he had gone from walking zombie to doubling his custom software firm and *working just 10 hours per week.* He spent the rest of his time on new business ventures and being with his family.

He earned this rich lifestyle by choosing to free up time to focus on building a real business that worked for him instead of continuing to be a slave to what was actually a very stressful job.

## Building leaders and relinquishing control gave him true freedom in his life and business.

It was such an incredible change for his family, too. His wife was able to quit her job to grow their family. Brandon experienced so much relief by creating a Hands-Off CEO business that gave him more wealth, freedom, and income.

Scaling this way allows you to choose how much or how little you want to work in your business. Your direct presence isn't needed for the business to run or grow.

What ultimately holds CEOs back from having this type of business is fear of making it worse. For Brandon, NOT building his business had trapped him. We were able to find the cash right within his company to make all these wonderful changes that gave him an incredible life.

**Change is hard. Not changing is harder.**

Brandon was given a polarizing gift where he was forced to change. He didn't have the option that most have, reasoning, "It's not so bad."

Do you want to create the life you want now? Or will you wait for conditions to force you to change?

I can tell you from interacting with over a thousand businesses in this space that most would become severely damaged if the CEO was out for two to six weeks, either physically from illness or emotionally from dealing with a personal loss.

The key to letting go of the Superman Complex and creating this peace of mind and freedom is a new focus. In Chapter 11, we'll look at your job #1 as the CEO.

# CHAPTER 11

# Your Job #1 as the CEO

*"Urgent things shout, important things whisper.*
*Listen to the whispers."*
*– Ken Groen*

Are you starting to see that your role in the business is shifting as the CEO?

At each new stage, your role and how you add value shift. The further you scale your company, the more valuable your time as CEO becomes. And the less it makes sense to work in the business versus on or above the business.

Let's first talk about what your job is not...

- Your job is *not* to manage clients
- Your job is *not* to build systems
- Your job is *not* to manage people
- Your job is *not* to run the hiring process

I'm not saying you're not going to be involved in these areas, but they cannot remain "your job" if you want to scale.

The kind of changes we're talking about don't happen overnight. From intense research, we've found five areas in the business you must exit from to create a more passive wealth-driven company.

Just the first three exits are business and life-changing, and for some, that's exactly where they want to be (detailed in Chapter 13). Those wanting to sell their business in the next five to seven years will want to pay close attention to all five of the exits to maximize the value of the business. These changes will make the business more enjoyable to own now and more attractive to an investor when you're ready to sell it which can literally mean walking away with millions more when you exit.

Your role as the CEO elevates as you safely let go and accomplish each exit. Every person in your organization should have a *Job #1*. Their most critical and important objective. Your role as the chief executive officer is no different.

## Your Job #1 as the CEO

Your job as a CEO is to expand, articulate, and enroll the team in the vision so that they are excited to execute it. It's to lead growth aligned with that vision and the core values you aspire to. It's to coach your team to do the work rather than doing it yourself.

Here is a piece that most business owners miss...

---

*Your job as the CEO is to build leaders who build the company.*

---

Otherwise, you're vastly underutilizing your talent. It's too bad most business owners miss this because it's the reason they are never able to generate the level of long-term wealth for themselves that they could have otherwise. That limits their ability to expand their impact in the world and reward their team.

Your job is defining the vision for where you're going, why you're going there, and who will be going along with you. It will define what roles to fill and the advisors that you need to guide your team.

You need to be able to articulate your vision of what you want and what success looks like so others around you can create that. They might have a different way of going about achieving that vision, which is good because they can make it better than you could have imagined.

Only when you can articulate what success looks like can you step back and let go of execution and control and be able to generate the same outcome.

Unfortunately, most CEOs are not clear enough in their vision. They know what they *don't* want but are unable to articulate what they *do* want. If you don't know what you want and where you want to go, how can your team take you there?

Knowing what you want, believing that what you want is possible, and believing that you're worthy of receiving it, is necessary to lead a team in accomplishing a huge vision.

Your business can only grow to the level that you, as a leader, have developed.

## The "HOW?" Mind Virus keeping you small

There's this paralyzing mind virus that can prevent us from reaching our full potential called... *"I don't know how."*

That last word, "how", keeps most CEOs stuck. They may have a big vision, but because they can't see "how" to achieve it, they get stuck or shrink their vision.

You don't need to know how. You really only get to see around the first bend. And it's a good thing because if you mapped it all out in detail over the next five years, market conditions, new opportunities, and life changes would force your plans to adjust, so why worry about every detail now?

**Let go of the fear of not knowing how.**

The "How Virus" is a scarcity cycle invented by the ego, designed to keep you in a tailspin so you don't venture too far from "safety."

Focus first on what you want to accomplish and why you want to do it. Then, the How will appear. The HOW will show up in the form of a WHO because you are clear on the WHAT and WHY.

Focusing on the How is a scarcity trap that will stop you more than anything else when you're looking to expand your business and your earning potential.

## Break Through the Ceiling

It really starts with going back to your vision and expanding it bigger than you. Take time every day to create your vision, asking, "What will my day look like?" Take time at the beginning of the quarter to ask, "What will my quarter look like?" Take time at the beginning of the year to ask, "What will my year look like?"

For years, I struggled with prioritizing visioning work. I thought that I just didn't have time to do it. *"I've got to DO this... and DO that, and also DO that, too... The vision stuff can wait!"*

And I was focused on all the wrong things because I was in the wrong headspace.

Mature leaders have an abundance mindset where they set aside a lot of time on their calendars for creating and visioning. It looks like open space.

Sometimes, the best creativity comes at times when you're not actually working. Your next level requires a lot of space.

If you want more abundance in your business and more financial abundance in your life, you need to create abundance in your calendar. You need to create space for it!

Align your investment of time and money with what you most want.

## Focus on the Important Work that Drives Growth

Have you ever had an employee who avoids certain tasks because they aren't confident they can do it well? They pass it off, don't take ownership, or procrastinate. What they really need is some encouragement, coaching, and perhaps some new skills.

It's the same for you as the CEO.

Become aware of when you avoid important work. Get the support you need to feel confident. Most importantly, feel the fear and do it anyway. Even if you fumble along the way, remember why you're doing it.

We've observed that there are certain stages where the CEO makes progress, then start jumping back into the details. During an uplevel... The "Hands-Off CEO Twitch" shows up as resistance or fear.

Jumping into familiar waters feels a whole lot safer than facing the uncertainty of all the new exciting things that come with scaling your business.

Get a team of smart "Vision Builders" in place, then trust them or find new people. Set criteria for what success looks and coach them to find their own answers.

Setting up leaders to win will help you safely let go. We'll talk specifically about how to do this in the next chapter.

Your ability to let go and trust is based on a few things. It's based on having the system in place, the people in place, and the frameworks in place. You need to have those things in place for you to be able to let go in a way that actually allows you to trust that the right work is moving forward. It's part system and part mindset, and you need both.

Covering both aspects allows you to emotionally let go of control and the significance that you were getting from having all the answers. Then being able to derive your significance from other places, like your personal life, coaching and developing people, expanding your vision, and impacting your community.

## Dissolving Fear

**Your Speed to Results is determined by your responses to and awareness of FEAR.** Some leaders are so entrenched in fear that it drives every action–and they are completely unaware of it!

Succumbing to fear stops action.

Fear never goes away. It's just made insignificant through a bigger vision. Fear is transcended by focusing on what you want and shifting the fear through aligned actions with vision.

We've had the great privilege of witnessing hundreds of meaningful transformations with our clients. Part of the leveling up process to realize these results is facing doubt and fear and flowing past it. When reasonable, and sometimes overwhelming, feelings come up, like "We don't have time now," "I can't do this," "I made a mistake," "I'm not ready," or "I don't think this is for me anymore..." This is often fear and resistance showing up.

In my experience, leaders react one of 3 ways:

1. **Fight/Flight** - challenge, push back, look for things that are wrong to give themselves permission to give up. REACT.
2. **Avoid/Delay** - get "busy," rework and rework, be "confused," look for reasons to delay. AVOID.
3. **Awareness/Ask for help** - sit with that feeling, get curious about it, name what is coming up, and reach out for support. ENGAGE.

How will you respond?

Leaders with the strongest businesses tend to live more in #3 as a result of the internal discipline they continue to master within themselves. From this place, they are able to powerfully coach their team to grow and do the same.

This is an important lesson you'll learn as you grow. You know the old saying..."New level, new devil."

Learning how to flow through these new levels with ease will make growth fun and rewarding rather than feeling like pushing a boulder up a hill while you stare down internal demons. We just get to develop self-awareness and learn how to lean in and sit with whatever is coming up without judgment.

**3 Key Questions to Focus on the Right Activities as the CEO:**

What is the most important activity I can do today to move my business forward?

What is the most important action I can take this week to expand my business?

What might my team need most from me to [outcome you want to achieve]?

Now that you know where to focus, let's transform your schedule–and free you up to create a resilient business that will weather the storms guaranteed to come in life. In Chapter 12, we'll cover two strategies that will free up ten extra hours per week to focus on growth.

# CHAPTER 12

# Free Up 10 Hours Per Week

*"Tell me what you value, and I might believe you, but show me your calendar and your bank statement, and I'll show you what you really value."*
*– Peter Drucker*

If you are looking for a quick win–here it is. Two simple shifts that will be the key to your next uplevel as a leader.

This solution will give you a jump start on the needed mindset, time, and mental bandwidth to implement a better plan to scale.

Time and money are the two common obstacles CEOs report for what stops them from fully embracing the Hands-Off CEO framework.

An effective scale strategy will remove obstacles from scaling — especially where those obstacles are imaginary. In Chapter 4, we covered finding cash and profit to scale. In the last two chapters, we talked about how your role changes as the CEO and how critical it is to lead your team to think differently so that you can experience different results. We talked about the shift from getting things done as a productive producer to *leading productivity through others.*

There is now a gap between where you should spend your time as a CEO versus how you are actually spending your time.

Now we'll free your time and close that gap creating space in your calendar to create at a new level.

I am going to show you how to reclaim at least 10 hours per week in the next seven to ten days. You can then invest that time into focused work on the business, accelerating profits. Or maybe that's just time that you want back for your family and personal projects. Either way, you win.

## What drives your day?

Most consulting companies and agencies are too busy to really take full advantage of growth opportunities. The company is stuck in a cycle of being reactively "busy, busy" because the CEO is too stuck working in the business. Many CEOs do not even have control over their own calendar.

We talk to CEOs all the time who have calendars packed to the brim with appointments. They badly need support to get some relief from the business and unlock the growth they know is there. But their calendars are so backed up that it takes weeks to get something scheduled. These are often the same CEOs who haven't had a real unplugged vacation in years.

What this ultimately means is that they don't have control over their own time.

**When you don't have control of your time, your business is driving you rather than you driving the business.**

There are two kinds of CEOs. The one who says, "Because this is important, I am going to block out time for it" and the other who lets others' priorities reactively drive their schedule. They use excuses like, "I can never meet at that time because I have standing client meetings."

Needing to have control over everything in the business, CEOs tend to lose control of the one thing that they need absolute control over… *their calendar.*

---

*If you don't have complete control over your calendar, you're an employee, not a CEO.*

---

Without control over your time, *you are the major obstacle and bottleneck to business growth.*

Your job as the CEO is to look ahead. To proactively look out for threats and envision ways to grow the business. But if you are too busy running your business (or it's running you), when will you have time to grow it?

**What's possible when you focus on the right things**

An agency we partnered with had great services, but the owner found himself stressed out being too involved in the day-to-day.

He was reluctant to grow too fast, fearing things would get worse because they didn't have the right team. Focusing his time on the right things allowed him to hire an operator to free him up for growth. He repositioned their offers to attract exceptional new clients. That gave them the cash flow to hire the right people to fix some of the root issues that kept the owners deeply involved in delivery.

All of this has lowered their stress and given them the peace of mind needed to scale. In just six months, they generated over $1 million of new revenue. The CEO now sees a simple path to growing the firm to $20 million in annual revenue.

We see big shifts like this all the time. You must focus on the most important activities if you want to lead growth in your business without working harder and harder.

## Shift #1: Supercharge Your Peak Time

The right plan will increase three very important freedoms: Time + Money + Location.

Increasing these freedoms in your life WHILE scaling up your business doesn't happen by accident.

Transforming your peak time into your Power Hour is your simple $1000/hr strategy that has the potential to start a chain reaction of positive outcomes in your company AND your life.

A chain reaction such as...

- Staff suddenly become more resourceful! Setting expectations with staff about when you are available and when you are not forces them to become more independent.
- Sets a consistent flow and framework to your day that lowers stress.
- Important work actually gets done because you're more effective and driven by priorities.

**Small hinges move big doors.**

One marketing agency executive started her day an hour earlier and blocked off the next 2 hours for uninterrupted, focused work. She recovered 15 productive hours per week or 60 per month. Half of the time she invested into business growth, and the other half she spent having fun with her husband.

The Power Hour is the most highly leveraged tweak that testing has shown to work universally for those who use it. You can start benefiting from it today, too.

How the Power Hour Works

Think of a time when you were in total flow. How much more were you able to accomplish than normal? How did it feel to roll out your best work at remarkable speed and efficiency?

We've found that every entrepreneur can achieve about 2X productivity in that state (some as much as 8x productivity). But you likely can't sustain that all day long.

When is your peak time?

For most people, their peak time is between 6:00 am and 11:00 am. These are commonly a person's best hours for focus. This graph shows a human's focus and alertness rhythm.

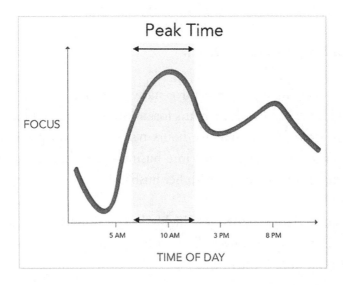

Some people are more productive later in the day. But it's important to note that existing habits like drug and caffeine use and sleep deprivation disrupt the natural circadian rhythm. Our environment dramatically impacts our performance and focus.

*"If we do not create and control our environment, our environment creates and controls us."*
*– Marshall Goldsmith*

Make any change to your environment that you need to that will result in a happier and more fulfilled life.

What have you noticed is your rhythm?

Have your assistant calendar a 1-2 hour Power Hour block for uninterrupted focus time. You'll get twice the work done in an hour. We've had CEOs report only needing to work half days because they complete all their work by noon.

## What might prevent you from finding your 20 extra hours per month?

As a recovering focus-challenged person, I know that focusing for long stretches can be difficult for some people. Aside from interruptions from staff and family, the biggest distractions can often be ourselves.

Do you even find yourself checking your email when you don't need to? Or pulled away to respond to something your team needs? As you sit down to do productive work, do you ever find that you need a drink or need to get up to use the restroom?

This is your mind resisting.

As long as you're not completely overworked, there is nothing wrong here. Awareness and redirecting yourself when you notice the resistance will build your focus muscle. And you'll be training yourself to focus for longer and longer stretches. Focus, just like anything else, is a muscle we build and master as we mature as leaders.

Visual cues like a notecard or planner can also help pull you back and clarify priorities.

## What could you do with 240 extra hours per year?

When you utilize one Power Hour per day, five days a week, with the ability to accomplish twice as much in that hour, you would have 20 extra productive hours per month. That's 240 extra hours per year or nearly 2.5 months of 8-hour work days per year!

What income growth could you create with that extra time? How would your business change if you spent that 240 extra hours per year on your own marketing? When calculating the opportunity costs, it can be in the millions of dollars.

## You run the business instead of the business running you

When this shift happens, you become more focused on driving your business forward. And you can create massive transformations in your business in a very short amount of time from the increased focus and effectiveness.

How to implement it:

At the end of the day, decide on the three outcomes you want to accomplish for the next day. On a notecard or the top of a physical planner, write those three things that will move your business forward so you don't lose focus and get pulled away by the dozens of demands you're bombarded with. Do this at the close of your day.

Doing it at the end of the day creates a division between your business and the rest of your life. You write your list. Clear your head. And leave all the business baggage in your office.

One successful entrepreneur we worked with had a business that had become his life. This strategy helped him channel his energy and focus in his day, then structure it in a way that flowed for him. He was able to work 20 hours less per week while accomplishing the same or more.

He completes his day at 5 pm, which changed his life. It's eliminated the regular burnout stretches that put him out of commission for months at a time.

What goes on the card?

Consider your three years and 12-month vision. What action could I take right now to make tangible progress toward that vision? What are my $1000/hour growth activities?

My preference is to use a written planner. You can download our *Power Hour Planner,* which includes a daily and weekly printable action plan on the resources page for this book at https://handsoffceobook.com/resources.

But what about the rest of your day? How do you deal with the insurmountable tasks that pile on your shoulders?

## Shift 2: Let Go of the Biggest Time & Energy Sucks.

The Work Elimination Matrix helps you sort out what only you should do and what to do with everything else. It allows you to root out the biggest time & energy sucks. This may take longer to transition into, but we find that all of our clients find a few tweaks that can make a difference right away.

### The Work Elimination Matrix

The Work Elimination Matrix is one of several tools we use to help companies grow beyond bottlenecks. In every business, there are bottlenecks to growth. How do you find these bottlenecks? You measure, then eliminate, automate, or delegate.

As the CEO, you are often the biggest bottleneck in the business, which means that to measure and get clarity on how to free your time, you need to track it. Here's how to do it:

Step 1: Track every activity you do for three days. No activity is too small or insignificant. If you do it, write it down.

Step 2: Next to each activity, write down which quadrant it falls in based on The Work Elimination Matrix below.

Step 3: "Reassign" each activity going forward based on which quadrant it's in.

Quadrant 1: You're doing it.
Quadrant 2: Delegate or automate it.
Quadrant 3: Eliminate, delegate, or automate.
Quadrant 4: Eliminate.

## The Work Elimination Matrix

Not your focus? *Eliminate, Automate, Delegate, and Consolidate.*

A practical warning

You might get some mixed responses to the changes you're leading. Some on your team will love them– "Finally, you are stepping out of onboarding and just letting us do our job!"

Not everyone around you will immediately like some of these changes. Your spouse might want a faster response to texts. (My husband found this annoying, but he's gotten over it now that he sees what I need to work effectively for a balanced life.) Your team coming up with solutions on their own instead of coming to you for the safe and "right" answer may be uncomfortable at first. Imagine how that could make them grow and stretch.

When we rock the boat, we often trigger others' fear (and often our own, too). People are naturally uncomfortable with both change and uncertainty. We need to be sensitive to this because, as entrepreneurs, we develop an abnormally high tolerance for uncertainty and risk compared to the rest of the population.

Often, we also attract mates who complement us with skills and experience opposite from our own. We want people in our business this way, too. But they may need reassurance, and most importantly, they need to hear your certainty and conviction in the chosen path forward.

It's your life and your business... own your time. Be intentional and disciplined about focusing on fewer activities that generate the biggest impact. It is the only path to greatness. It's also the key to your freedom: making more, working less.

This personal skill set is important for you to model for your leaders. In the next Chapter we'll break down the 5 CEO Exits and what to delegate next for the biggest impact when scaling a service.

# PART 4

## Double Team Growth Capacity

# CHAPTER 13

# The 5 CEO Exits

What you did in Chapter 12 to free your time is all about working with what you have. If you followed the steps, you have freed up an extra 10 hours per week. You're refocused on what's more important, eliminating distractions, delegating things that you don't need to do, and empowering your team to share more of the load.

To clear your plate, you start with administrative and piecemeal work, including sales admin (not selling yet...we'll get there). Next, you'll strategically exit parts of the business by hiring and developing leaders to take over chunks of your current workload.

You've probably read other books that promise to show you how to gain freedom and scale your business. What's new here is the sequencing of the exits specifically for custom services. There is nuance to it, which is why we've seen such consistency with this sequencing pattern.

Systematically let go, one area at a time, and in the order laid out in this chapter. Many are tempted to skip ahead. Don't.

From over a decade of research consulting with hundreds of agency owners, following the process will save you time, money, and frustration. It works consistently across consulting businesses.

On the rare occasion we've seen a good reason to slightly adjust the order based on existing skills and strengths in the business, the implementation is clunky. It's still better to follow the process because each exit builds the systems, mindsets, and skills needed for the following exit.

## Growth increases the workload

Instead of the CEO continuing to absorb more and more responsibility as the business grows, we're going to shift the ownership for key areas of the business from you onto the leaders you develop.

There are five main leadership areas to exit to create sustainable hands-off growth. They fit within three main growth phases, building upon each step to create an increasingly valuable hands-off business.

These 5 exits exist within 3 main phases of growth.

1) Build Capacity
2) Scale Growth
3) Passive Asset

You'll notice that the 3 phases build on top of the 'Foundations to Scale' covered in part two of this book. This foundation is what makes these exits sustainably work. Let's now look at how what exit to prioritize to generate the most ease in your business based on how your time is currently allocated.

## Solid Foundation to Scale an 8-Figure Consultancy

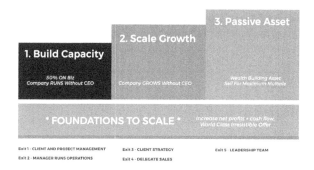

## Identify Your Current Benchmark

Consider your current schedule. How many hours per week do you work on average? How is your time divided between different functions in your business?

| CEO TIME PERCENTAGE<br>**What Percentage of Your Time**<br>Do you spend in Each Area of the Business? | % | *Hours per Week* |
|---|---|---|
| **1 - Client Service & Project Management**<br>*Client communication, meetings, and implementing project timelines.* | | |
| **2 - Operations Management**<br>*Managing team to implement the vision, scorecards, quarterly goals, running team meetings, and streamlining systems.* | | |
| **3 - Client Strategy**<br>*Skilled strategic work and client strategy sessions. (Not day to day implementation meetings)* | | |
| **4 - Sales & Marketing**<br>*Business development, sales closing, marketing strategy, speaking, partnerships.* | | |
| **5 - Executive Leadership**<br>*Strategic planning, innovation, vision, coaching leaders.* | | |
| **TOTAL** | | |

What do you notice about your numbers? Do any trends pop out? Which area generates the biggest growth impact? Which areas are you spending the most time in?

**The more you focus on the last two areas, the more growth you can generate.**

Repeat after me:

---

*"The less I work in my business, the more money I make."*

---

Pin it on your wall and read it aloud every day.

Compare your numbers to the following chart that benchmarks the percentage of time the CEO spends in each part of the business based on each successful exit stage.

| CEO TIME BENCHMARKS | | | | | | |
|---|---|---|---|---|---|---|
| Percentage of Time CEO Spends in Each Part of Business Based on Each Successful Exit Stage | | | | | | |
| CEO Leadership Exits | Typical Before | 1 | 2 | 3 | 4 | 5 |
| 1 - Client Service & Project Management | 40% | 5% | 2% | 2% | 2% | 2% |
| 2 - Operations Management | 20% | 18% | 3% | 3% | 3% | 3% |
| 3 - Client Strategy | 22% | 22% | 25% | 10% | 10% | 5% |
| 4 - Sales & Marketing | 13% | 50% | 50% | 60% | 5% | 3% |
| 5 - Executive Leadership | 5% | 5% | 20% | 25% | 80% | 88% |
| How CEO Exits Impacts Total Time Worked Per Week in Business. | | | | | | |
| Average Range of Hours Per Week | 50-60 | 40-50 | 30-40 | 20-30 | 10-20 | 1-5 |

Note that as the CEO moves through the 5-Exits, their overall time burden in the business reduces as well. This means that while you may be spending 88% of your time in executive leadership at the end, your overall time working in the business is reduced dramatically.

## The 5 Exits Shift You From "Doer" to "Leader"

Your time and focus change as you become a Hands-Off CEO. You move increasingly from doer and problem solver to leader and coach as you progress through each exit.

Your team needs you to communicate your vision of what success looks like and then be held to set standards and agreements. You're telling them what and why, not how. You'll be thrilled to see what is possible when their time, energy, and creativity are applied to implementing your inspiring vision.

## Exit 1 - Client Service & Project Management

***Operationalize your Irresistible Offer to win back 10-20 more hours per week***

The first exit is client support and project management. We see this free up to 10 to 20 hours per week for the CEO. This is draining work that doesn't need to be done by you.

But many CEOs see this as the hardest exit because if it's not done right, quality drops, and the business will lose clients and revenue. This exit is so hard because client support, project management, fulfillment, and client strategy all get lumped together. It's like employing a surgeon to input patient records, take vitals, and make a diagnosis— all at once.

You need to split this role apart to best utilize talent and increase output. Otherwise, you backlog your highest-level people with work that's far below their pay grade. This is not sustainable as it eats up the capacity of your best people.

**One of the simplest and most cost-effective ways to increase capacity is to backfill work for your top people by building out processes and having them train their replacements.**

Do this by operationalizing your *Irresistible Offer* and Client Success Map. In this step, operations leaders take their clearly defined offer and outcome as laid out in the Client Success Map, then break it down into milestones, KPIs, and clear processes. This defines at least 80% of the whole end-to-end process from onboarding to the next engagement. It's key to remove yourself from client management without each and every project being a totally custom roadmap—which is what keeps you stuck in client communication. Because you're the only one who can actually make sure it gets done that way.

Freeing up first yourself, then your other leaders, as you continue to scale, allows space for continual growth and proactive business improvement. Freeing your leaders to become bigger profit centers makes it easier for the company to justify paying them more. Win-win.

Momentum builds as you start seeing the rewards from laying these foundations. You have more freedom to grow your business in ways that seemed impossible while you were still personally delivering on every project. It also sets up a manager to effectively run the operations.

## Exit 2 - Operations Management

### Double Your Capacity By Empowering Your Operations Leader

To truly take a step back from working in your business to finally work on it, you need a manager to take care of running the day-to-day business.

Without this person, you're stuck reacting to every little thing that could possibly demand your attention, leaving you drained and pulling your focus from what you should be working on.

An effective operations leader who fits your values and culture frees you to grow the business and ensures that your team is profitably running your business—even when you aren't there.

Many CEOs in this transition wonder, "What should I expect this person to do?"

**The five key responsibilities of your operations leader:**

1. Leading the team in **turning your vision into a reality.** They can ground your big ideas and help translate them into actionable plans for the rest of the company.
2. **Solve problems before you're even aware of them.** From small issues that take 15 minutes to solve to bigger problems that could derail an entire month, your operations manager can make them disappear.
3. **Profitably run the business based on repeatable systems.** Read that sentence again, as it's critical. They can even lead the team in innovating and improving these systems.
4. **Improve quality for clients.** As your company grows, your operations leader will improve your team's ability to deliver outcomes.
5. **Manage your team for you** measured against your vision and specific scorecards for each role. This gives your team more support and breaks one of the biggest bottlenecks in your business.

From research working with hundreds of services and consulting agency CEOs, we found that most operators need development to meet the demands of your growing company related to these five responsibilities. **This position has a high failure rate. It is VERY EASY to get wrong!**

While it's common that there's a gap, this doesn't mean you have the wrong person.

If you have someone already filling the role, start by sharing this list with them to make a plan to fully step into this role. The right person will enjoy the growth opportunity and will appreciate you setting the bar for what's expected so you both have clear criteria for success. It also helps the CEO to butt out so the team can do their jobs. (There will be many operations leaders who read that last line and cheer.)

Achieving this level of performance with your chief bottleneck-breaker is absolutely critical for finding the time, space, and profits you need to grow your business to its full potential. Finding the right person and empowering them is one of the biggest things we see missing from our clients as they scale. Does this have to be one person? No. At first, one person will oversee these 5 roles. As the company grows, the roles branch out and become more specialized. How the role is divided up will depend on the gaps in existing resources.

Without this key piece in place, you're stuck both growing and managing the business. Not having this management layer in place is what keeps service businesses stuck in the lower 7 figures.

Common Mistakes - Hiring the right talent so you can safely let go!

- **Hiring an operations leader who cannot match your desired pace!** This is a common issue we see. Operations leaders naturally tend to be slower and more methodical, which is a good thing. But you'll both go crazy if your pace is too far off. Also, being vague about implementation timelines, having excuses for missed deadlines, and being unable to lead hard conversations about team performance will slow organizational pace– which will slow execution for the entire team.

- **Hiring a highly experienced person who isn't willing to get their hands dirty.** They may have solid operations leadership experience at a bigger firm. But they also need the ability, willingness, and flexibility to work with limited resources to turn chaos into calm. Be careful if they are from an environment where all of the systems, teams, and processes already exist. For them, coming into your business will be like moving from the pristine penthouse into the middle of a renovation project. It's going to be beautiful one day soon, but **you need someone who will roll up their sleeves to actually build out the vision alongside your team!**

- **Abdicating responsibility to an experienced but uncoachable manager.** Entrusting your business to a person who's unwilling to take feedback is a nightmare waiting to happen. They could be very effective but can drive your business in a different direction than you want.

It's possible to be shifted with an empowering conversation. But lacking humility means they aren't teachable, which means they can't grow.

- **Not knowing what success looks like and not having clear expectations to manage.** In this case, even exceptional talent will get frustrated and may leave. The five key expectations earlier in this chapter solve this.

- **Lacking an effective framework to operationalize a custom services business.** Even skilled operators need training on the best practices for a custom service business model like yours. It's not like other businesses they may have worked in, and there are few resources available to learn the model. You need a different systems approach to successfully operate the business.

Avoiding these mistakes and getting your operations leader to take on the five key responsibilities takes the pressure off the CEO, which makes it possible to generate growth without needing to work harder.

We've had clients literally add 7-figures of growth to their businesses in 12 months or less because their team was able to step up and take ownership. The operations leader supported the growth by independently running the day-to-day business. That allowed the CEO to work their magic in growing the company.

## Exit 3 - Client Strategy

*Clone key strategic roles to scale.˘*

This is where we take all of the work you've done and bring it to more people. That is not so easy to do. Let's look at why it can be hard and how you can develop talent within a fraction of the time.

Grant shared this frustration about the efforts they had made to transfer knowledge internally.

*"Even people who are already very technical need a lot of additional time to get up to speed on our specific niche. As soon as a team member hits their stride and is really competent, the demands on their time from clients and the rest of the team become immense. Getting them to be effective at turning their knowledge into reusable training has been a very slow grind.*

*The team understands the need, but we just have a huge collection of 20% finished stuff because of just how much there is to cover. We're trying to figure out what an official streamlined repeatable process might look like, and it's really time-consuming and distracts us from immediate client needs.*

*The struggle has absolutely been figuring out where that 20% that provides 80% of the ROI. And we keep coming back to seemingly irreducible complexity in the sense that any missing piece breaks the whole."*

**The real problem is a lack of focus.**

To scale strategy, you need one standardized proven process for a single, focused, ideal client type. That's where the Client Success Map comes in.

To scale that, you must have a standardized, proven process that allows you to attract top talent to build out the execution of your process.

The CEO doesn't build the processes. They lead and coach the team to build up the processes. Then, your top talent develops junior team members, allowing you to grow talent internally.

This is where *Apprenticeship Programs* come in.

Apprenticeship programs are a self-perpetuating talent development system. As you scale, you'll always have new talent to backfill and handle the growth.

This is the opposite of what most consulting agencies do, and it's why they struggle to staff growth. Most are hiring high-level talent throughout the company. That's very difficult to do as finding top talent is hard, and it's an extremely expensive and unsustainable way to scale.

No matter the skill level you hire, they still need training on the special way your organization does things. Sometimes the more training they have, the more retraining is needed.

### What Apprentice Training Programs Do You Need?

There are some roles where you'll need multiple people performing the same function. Think account management, project management, or certain fulfillment roles. For these repeatable roles, consider the main components new staff will need to master to be successful.

Then, map out a success path with milestones along the way where you can assess each person's mastery of the key skills. Then, you're able to pair junior team members with mentors who can "apprentice" them, ensuring they meet each of your standards as they develop.

The key for you as the CEO is to know that your senior leaders are the ones who build out this talent development system. You provide the vision and oversight, but they should be developing the program, implementing the training, and holding junior team members to your company standards.

With a system and culture of internal apprenticeship, you'll overcome the #1 limiter of growth– your ability to manufacture your own talent. Investing in your staff in this way becomes a compelling benefit to working for your company. Top talent will love that you removed obstacles to their success, creating an environment for growth.

## Exit 4 - Delegate Sales

*Scale sales by training sales strategists so the company can grow without you.*

Less mature CEOs tend to jump ahead to this exit because sales is time-consuming and full of rejection. The foundations for delegating sales are discussed in Chapters 7-9.

If you'd like to start here, go ahead... if and ONLY IF you like flushing money down the toilet. If you haven't done the work to create your Irresistible Offer and simplified your selling system using a Client Success Map, you're not going to like this experience.

Without the proper foundations, you'll be gambling on a sales superstar to come in and "take it all off your plate." Not only will it take you countless hours to train on all the complexities of your bespoke offerings, but it will also take at least six months to see if they can test, innovate, and install the needed sales systems to consistently generate sales. All while they happily take a six-figure base salary to figure it out.

**The best sales professionals want an environment where they can win.**

They aren't afraid of stretching to hit quotas and KPIs because they like making a lot of money. But, even if you luck out with a top sales producer, they won't stay long working for a business with weak offers and undefined sales processes.

The right foundations allow you to scale profits, not just client volume. You can otherwise pay a very high acquisition cost for the wrong sales that actually hurt the business.

There are a lot simpler ways to initially grow your sales without the added complexity of a sales team.

When we take our clients through the Irresistible Offer Intensive in the earlier stages of working together, we create a simple Go-to-Market growth strategy to build on what's already working. Capacity is limited, so we focus on referrals, follow-up, and accelerating existing channels.

What we do is set the bar higher with prospects and stop wasting time with those who won't be stellar clients or who aren't yet ready. Then reinvest the time in creating assets and case studies that educate prospects and position market expertise. .

**This simple focus will shorten the sales cycle and attract more of the right high-profit clients.**

As you are hands-on improving sales effectiveness, sales admin support can help you accomplish more in less time. Best practices are standardized into a *Sales Playbook* that allows you to attract top sales talent who love your vision and respect your proven sales model that they can improve upon.

Your *Sales Playbook* and your *Apprenticeship Program* laid out in Exit 3, come together to turn an effective sales closer into a respected *sales strategist* that your clients will trust.

To safely exit this role, hire a professional with a track record of success, systematically trained on your unique approach for consulting with clients. Build a leader who you can effectively transfer trust so that you can scale sales without you being the only one driving growth.

## Exit 5 - Executive Leadership

*Strategic planning, innovation, vision, coaching leaders.*

Many CEOs aren't interested in exiting this part of the business at this time. They want to spend more of their time in this area with the option to exit the business completely when they are ready, which is usually years away.

At this stage, you may need more senior C-suite roles as the company expands. Those leaders will be coaching and developing less senior leaders, and you'll be mentoring your C-Suite.

The very last thing to let go of is the vision and direction of your company, looking ahead for threats and ways to innovate to stay competitive in the market.

This last stage allows for complete freedom and wealth actualization as you have an asset that operates and grows without your involvement in the business operations at all. You've moved from owner/operator to investor. The business is now positioned to be sold as a lucrative asset for other investors.

At this stage, you'll hire a CEO to replace you. We have had clients groom a COO internally over several years to take over as CEO when the client exited to work on other ventures.

What exit would you like to reach as your ultimate goal in your business?

In the final chapter of this book, I've laid out a detailed checklist that encompasses everything covered in this book so far, including the exits. What you have now is ultimate freedom and options that you can act on from a place of strength. It's the pinnacle of business success for the few who reach this milestone.

In the next chapter, I'll show you how to turn your team into profit centers and let go – safely and with confidence...

# CHAPTER 14

# How to Turn Your Team into Profit Centers

Perry enjoyed 367% growth over three years as he replaced himself in Exits 1, 2, and most of Exit 3. He had dramatically decreased his stress level from a few years earlier. Yet, year after year, Perry would overbook his schedule with legacy client engagements that he had close relationships with. He wanted to grow and could see adding at least a million dollars of new business if he could just spend more time selling and speaking.

I asked how much revenue the legacy clients were worth altogether. $300k.

*"Let's say, worst case scenario, they all fire you, and you lose $300k. But you added $1M. Is it worth $700k to make that change knowing you'd actually be working less?"*

That's just year one. A quick calculation would show with their rate of possible growth, it would be at least $3-5M of missed revenue over the next few years. Not to mention, new clients came in paying more and didn't expect the CEO.

Perry enjoyed working with those clients, but he had a decision to make about what was more important: the significance of working in the business or the lifestyle he wanted where he could travel with his wife and work fewer hours as he nears retirement age.

With each of the 5 Exits, there is a corresponding mindset shift that allows you to let go.

---

*When you assign a leader to take over a chunk of your workload and find yourself still very involved, they either aren't owning it, or you have not let go.*

---

At that point, the CEO must ask, "Which is it? Have they not owned it, or have I not let go?"

At each of the 5 Exits, letting go requires more courage and trust. That requires a new mindset shift as you approach each exit.

You are moving from "Doer" to "Leader." From someone who gets things done through your own productivity and effort to someone who gets things done through the work of others. You become a problem solver and coach for your team, and they need you to assume that new role.

The team needs the CEO to develop a clear vision, then communicate it. They need to hear from the CEO, "This is what success looks like," with standards and accountability needed to reach success. When you shift to the role of leader and clearly communicate the vision, your team is empowered to take your vision and apply their own creativity to it. Often, our client CEOs are excited and surprised by how much better the team executes when they bring their own creative thought and energy to their work.

---

*When you've hired the right people, the systems are set up, and you still find yourself being pulled in, then...*

*You're the problem, sweetheart. ;)*

---

Here are some questions to consider:

"Where do I add value to the business?"
"What would happen if I just didn't do this ___ anymore?"
"Where am I most passionate about spending my time?"
"Where might there be misalignment with my values and goals?"

### Letting go in stages through sequential exits

There are several layers of letting go. As we see with Perry, you safely let go by going through the exits sequentially. You build on each stage as your business matures. Get out of the day-to-day in stages so you don't disrupt results and so you can increase client experience and the consistency of outcomes.

It's not all or nothing. You securely and intentionally let out the rope, a little bit at a time.

### *Safely* let go of control

Hands-Off CEO leadership allows you to get a lot more done with less of your time but requires a lot more intention. It requires letting go to pour your time and energy into building those around you to do the work better than you could.

I can't even tell you the gratification I find from watching my team build and execute my vision of the Hands-Off CEO movement. They bring levels of innovation that I couldn't have dreamed up on my own.

These are effective leaders on their own, but with your mentorship, they rise to whole new levels. They do the best work of their career and rise to meet the high standards of your brand. Imagine what would be possible if you had a business full of these kinds of leaders!

Even if you feel like you're far away from that now, know that you can have this if you choose to create it. You can start by shifting your current team. Raise the bar in an encouraging way that excites them to be part of what you're building.

## Turf Builders or Vision Builders

Some won't rise to the new bar you set. Some will rise for a while, then hit their upper limit and stall out. These people will show their true identities as turf builders, not the vision builders that you need to take your organization to the next level.

Todd found himself in this place with a key project leader. He was faced with a painful choice: live with it and continue the pattern of mediocrity in his business or rip off the Bandaid and deal with the issue head-on right in the middle of their busy season.

He chose to do the latter, and it lit a fire under him. He took his stale job ad that for months had been up receiving only weak responses. He took that fire and rewrote it to attract the talented vision builders he wanted. He got two solid applicants in one day and hired one right away.

This took a leap of faith for Todd. The choice he made won't be right for all businesses. Some may want a more gradual transition. But Todd found that doing this was a catalyst that shifted deeply worn patterns that kept him stuck in the business, earning too little profit for the long hours that he was working.

That's the power of taking a stand for your vision and being intentional about building it.

## Setting Leaders Up to Win

When hiring and training for a new role, we often go between two extremes.

**Micromanage**                                    **Abdicate**

1) **Micromanage** - If you go the micromanaging route, you may as well do the thing yourself. You're acting as the puppet master. They never develop the confidence to own it. This approach creates learned helplessness and dependence on you.
2) **Abdicate** - "You go do it and figure it out." This is setting up the person to sink or swim without the support they

need to be successful. They cannot meet your standards, and you'll have to jump in to fix it or constantly give feedback.

Both approaches set up good people to fail. They don't allow the person to develop the confidence to own the role because they haven't been empowered to do so.

They become frustrated, and good people may leave for a position at another firm where they can actually win. Over time, you'll lose your best, most capable people and be left with a team of puppets. No matter how skilled a person is, they'll have mediocre performance because they haven't been set up to win. It will be virtually impossible to determine if your people are competent or not because they're just doing what you tell them to do.

You've essentially said to them, "I only want your hands, not your brain. I'll do all the thinking for you." This is not a path to CEO freedom.

This doesn't mean you have to have all your ducks perfectly in a row to set high expectations of your people.

Moving from the extremes of abdication or micromanagement to an outcome-based, leader-led management approach is the keystone shift a CEO must make for any of the five exits to work. It means clearly defining success in agreements in your business. Then managing those agreements rather than managing the person. It takes intention, but it allows you to be fair and empowering.

Without this shift, there is no freedom for you. It is the essence of the trap that most service firm owners find themselves in. When you make the mindset shift, you'll immediately begin to accelerate growth while working less and delivering increasingly better outcomes for clients.

## Can they take "too much" ownership?

Anna was drowning. Her company was bursting at the seams, and they could no longer sell. She was working 60+ hours per week and not sleeping enough, which was becoming a huge stress on her body.

She was relieved when her friend Mary, who had exceptional operations skills, offered to come in and help. Mary came well recommended and quickly whipped things into shape. She brought order and structure to the company, and Anna was thrilled to be able to take on more clients. But it was all now dependent on Mary.

Mary had built her own kingdom and was swapping Anna's vision with her own. She began making important decisions without consulting Anna. She went so far as to launch new products that weren't aligned with the company. Then, she elevated her title to COO and demanded more pay.

This is an extreme example. Most situations are more subtle with leaders who have more honorable intentions.

Support your leaders to delegate their massive workloads as you have. Coach them to build out their role to be repeatable. It's good for their stress level and prevents a 'key man' scenario where one person still has all the keys to the castle– and it's not you.

**Prevent unhealthy dynamics from taking root in the team.**

If cultural dysfunction already exists, it will worsen until properly addressed *by the CEO*. You can shift it by expanding your vision, boldly resetting the bar, and rallying everyone around a shared vision. Then you have a team of enthusiastic, vision-builder profit centers. Meanwhile, those without the shared vision tend to self-select out.

Next, in our final Chapter, we'll leave you with *The Consulting Agency Scalability Checklist* that gives you the key actions to implement these expansive changes into your business.

# The Consulting Agency Scalability Checklist

*"Two roads diverged in a wood, and I—*
*I took the one less traveled by,*
*And that has made all the difference."*
*– Robert Frost*

You've put so much of yourself into this business. It's come at the cost of years of missed events with your kids and late nights away from your spouse. It's likely come with a lot of stress and even neglecting your own health and hobbies. Months of not taking a paycheck. Years of not getting paid what you are really worth.

It was all worth it to build this amazing company you have. But now is the time to leverage what you've built to fully monetize your brilliance and grow beyond yourself. All while giving opportunities for income growth and freedom to the families of those who work for your business.

You may find yourself in this weird middle ground where you have good people in place but lack the internal infrastructure to connect all the dots. Now is the time to empower your team to take what you've created and make it far better than you could do on your own.

It's time to define your vision and your expectations for your team, then let go and allow them to rise to their full potential.

Refocusing your time to focus on leveraged growth. Identifying and securing higher-level clients to replace low-paying, low profitability clients will allow you to scale sustainably. Get paid what you are worth by helping clients recognize the value your team delivers. Simplify your selling process so that you have a tangible and repeatable premium product that can be delivered consistently and sold for maximum profit... And also can be sold *without you.*

Maybe you know you can reach your growth goals by continuing to do what you are doing, but when you are in the thick of it, will you hate your life getting there? At what point will that stop you?

Taking the right steps, in the right order, will allow you to reach that pinnacle of business success while retaining your sanity.

Imagine a team of leaders and doers who allow you to safely let go. Imagine your time freed up to seek out other opportunities, either to grow this company or expand other burning ideas you have.

## Philip Did It and So Can You

Philip Nickerson's path to half the hours and 6X growth.

When we met, Philip was working an insane schedule to keep up with demands while traveling all over the Canadian Maritime Provinces. There were plenty of opportunities for growth, but not without more stress and more hours. It was already a challenge for his young family.

Before becoming a Hands-Off CEO, Philip's time was constantly **consumed with working IN the business.** There was no time to grow the business. His expertise was so specialized that he was very involved in service delivery. There was also a limited budget to hire a high-investment role they needed to expand.

Constantly on the move, he was just trying to keep up.

### Philip's Transformation

**Philip first found more time.** Nothing was going to change until he was freed up to actually work ON his business. We helped him find three tweaks to quickly uncover *90 extra hours per month* to work on his business. He eliminated 38 overnight job site trips per year so he was able to be with his family more. And he empowered his team to **make decisions without him.**

We worked through what it would take to install a new delivery system without any breakdowns. He looked at everywhere it could go wrong and created a startup checklist so things would go off without a hitch. This dramatically lowered the level of expertise needed to consistently deliver a quality service. And with *a lot less of Philip.*

## What Philip accomplished

- Eliminated the need to hire another engineer, saving $100k per year in payroll.
- Freed up **90 extra hours per month** to spend with his family and invest back into the business.
- Delegated the most time-consuming parts of projects that he dreaded.
- **The Company grew 3.5X in one year – mostly utilizing his current team.**
- $100,000 of extra profit in the following year in just the first quarter.
- **The Company has grown beyond $4 million with new initiatives that continue to expand growth.**
- He enjoys a lot more time with his family, **can take weeks off with zero impact on his business,** and enjoyed a dream vacation with his wife to Scotland.
- **He now owns a "Hands-Off CEO Ecosystem" of companies that run without him.**

Becoming a Hands-Off CEO is possible with a big vision for innovation and exceptional service. Even if you have serious challenges with finding and training technical staff to meet growth demands like Philip and many of our clients have.

## But most CEOs will never have this kind of business and life.

Few have the courage to leave behind what has been working up to this point.

Next-level growth doesn't actually take more time. It takes realigning your priorities. It takes focus and courage. It takes choosing the path "less traveled by" that will make "all the difference."

## Few have the 'Courage to Create.' Do you?

Courageous growth feels good– but only after you face the fear and take the leap. The fear never goes away. It just gets drowned out by your commitment to something greater.

**Who are you willing to become to create the business and life that you desire?**

What could be possible if you created what you actually want as if you couldn't fail?

What if you could have a dramatic increase in growth AND lifestyle freedom?

You can have both, but you'll need to embody INTENSE courage, commit to the process, and focus on your vision. Especially on the days when it feels like it's not working– *it takes time to turn the ship.*

**Those who don't take this leap continue to be the bottleneck to growth, with endless decisions and responsibilities piling up on their desks.**

Will this be your life? How many more years will you allow your business to be all-consuming while your family silently resents your lack of full presence in their lives?

I know I am cutting deep, but I have lived it and found a way out! I want that for you too.

The life of the CEO sucks when you're filling in the gaps where others aren't fully owning it.

**Now** is the time to get control of your business by stepping back and empowering your team to take ownership. **Now** is your time to reclaim your freedom and say goodbye to being sucked back into the day-to-day. **Now** is your time to enjoy more stability in your business with a concrete plan in place to fund retirement. Now is your time to transform your years of hard work and financial investment into personal wealth and legacy.

To stop being the hands-on person doing day-to-day chores and calls that aren't the best use of your time as the CEO. To safely let go of the tactical work and instead spend your time on the strategic high-value work that is fun and grows the business.

**Most CEOs know they are missing out on big opportunities because of limited bandwidth.**

The pressure is on to keep up with the backlog of work that piles onto your plate. Because if you don't deliver, it's going to negatively impact your business. It's going to damage the good reputation that you have if delivery starts to slip.

Our clients work with us so that they don't have to carry that burden alone. So that they have a partner who can see around the corner and help them prevent costly mistakes. To give them a roadmap to get there faster with the people and systems in place to be sustainable and grow profits as they scale. To feel good about how clients are treated as the CEO lets go. To have a path that they are confident in to continue to grow the business beyond them.

**How much growth would be possible if your team could deliver excellent results without your *involvement*?**

If it were possible for you to double growth while working less, how might you approach your business differently??

It is possible for you. Will you step into your new future?

Do not fall for the lie we often tell ourselves that *"no one can do it as well as I can."* It's just not true, if… you choose a focused growth path, to scale an exceptional service with an *Irresistible Offer*. And if you operationalize the process into a *Service Management Blueprint* and systematically clone your expertise with a proprietary *Apprentice Training Program*.

That's the right step to make it happen and add millions of sustainable growth without killing yourself to get there. It is work, but you're already working hard and not getting to where you want, as fast as you want. This path gives you the cash flow and profit margins so that you don't have to do it alone.

On the following pages is a checklist to safely exit yourself from parts of the business that drain your energy and stagnate growth. This is key to increasing service quality by replacing yourself with skilled leaders who can give each role the attention it deserves.

## The Consulting Agency Scalability Checklist

*This checklist shows you The Profitable Foundations to Scale, and what roles to delegate, in what order.*

These roles can be employee, contractor, fractional, or outsourced to freelance specialists or agencies. Delegation across previous exits is ongoing as your company evolves. This is not a comprehensive list. For a printable version of this Consulting Agency Scalability Checklist, go to https://handsoffceobook.com/resources

### PROFITABLE FOUNDATIONS TO SCALE

*The CEO is responsible for driving this.*

- ☐ **Growth & Exit Plan** - Evaluate your current growth stage and what you need to reach the next level.
- ☐ **Find Time NOW!** - Free up 10 hours per week to invest in growth.
- ☐ **Install Execution Foundation** - Accountability structure to manage change and execute the CEO's vision:
  - ☐ Quarterly and annual growth plans.

- ☐ Structure and meeting rhythms to manage staff to their job description and quarterly strategic objectives.
- ☐ Raise the Bar conversation to create a culture of accountability.
- ☐ **Irresistible Offer** - Command a 50-600% higher price point.
  - ☐ Define the right growth with an Irresistible Offer to double gross profits.
  - ☐ Simple Go-to-Market Growth Strategy.

## CLIENT EXECUTION & BUSINESS OPERATIONS EXITS

*Leaders are responsible for managing the areas of the business below.*

- ☐ **Task and Client Execution** (Find Time NOW! Exit 1)
  - ☐ Delegate specific parts of client projects following detailed processes, or outsource to skilled producers.
- ☐ **Client Service / Account Management**
  - ☐ Delegate client communication and project management. (Exit 1)
  - ☐ Standardize 80% of delivery by operationalizing *Client Success Map* into *Service Management Blueprint*. (Exit 2)
- ☐ **Ops Leader** - Manage Profitability, Quality, and Increase Capacity (Exit 2)
  - ☐ Lead the team to turn your vision into reality.
  - ☐ Drive accountability with the five key responsibilities of your operations leader.
- ☐ **Client Strategy** - (Exit 3)
  - ☐ Clone your expertise.

    ☐ Build expert strategists from within with an Apprentice Training Program.

## GROWTH EXITS

☐ **Delegate Sales** - (Exit 4)
    ☐ Refine Go-to-Market Growth Strategy.
    ☐ Define Sales Playbook.
☐ **Senior Leadership** - C-Suite roles as company scales (Exit 5)
    ☐ CFO, CTO, CMO (fractional to start with, moving into full-time roles as needed)
    ☐ COO, CEO

# Next Steps: Ever Expanding Growth and Freedom

## The Hands-Off CEO™ Program

Discover a gateway to ever-expanding growth and freedom... To a business that fulfills all of the dreams you have for yourself, for your family, for your team, and for your clients. That business and life is possible for you. We've built our Hands-Off CEO™ programs to give you the guidance and support to get there without the trial and error, the struggle, and the frustration that most CEOs go through.

When you're ready to begin living in bigger freedom, with more abundance that allows you to make a much bigger impact, here is what to do next...

Would you like to be our next big client success story?

At the time of publication, we have 3 ways we work with consulting agencies to scale profitably.

1) *Irresistible Offer Intensive* - 12-week program to get the right offer in place, the right pricing model to scale, and a Client Success Map that forms the foundation for your team to build the company on. This is the powerful foundation that connects all the processes in this book. This process helps consulting agencies command dramatically higher fees with an elevated service that clients are eager to buy.

2) *Scale to Freedom* - comprehensive 12-month program for CEOs and their operators covering the contents of this book, including foundations to scale and Exits 1-4.

Qualifying CEOs have established teams, and finding new business is not their biggest challenge. This support both removes the CEO from the day-to-day, and enables millions of dollars of profitable sustainable growth.

3) *Board of Advisors* - for Scale to Freedom graduates building 8-9 figure companies, scaling Tech-Enabled Services, or otherwise working toward a lucrative business exit.

If you would like our help to implement the proven strategies outlined in this book into your business, apply to have a complimentary Scalable Growth Session with my team. We'll assess your situation and help you to see possibilities in your situation. If it looks like a good fit, we'll share options to partner together to help you *Scale to Freedom*!

https://www.handsoffceo.com/scale